W9-CHI-505

John Gray

Twayne's English Authors Series

Herbert Sussman, Editor
Northeastern University

TEAS 353

JOHN GRAY
(1866–1934)
Photo Courtesy: Dr. Paul Winckler

John Gray

By G. A. Cevasco
St. John's University

Twayne Publishers • *Boston*

John Gray

G. A. Cevasco

Book production by John Amburg
Book design by Barbara Anderson

Printed on permanent/durable acid-free
paper and bound in The United States
of America.

Library of Congress Cataloging in Publication Data

Cevasco, G. A. (George A.)
  John Gray.

  (Twayne's English authors series; TEAS 353)
  Bibliography: p. 156
  Includes index.
  1. Gray, John, 1866-1934—Criticism and interpretation.
I. Title. II. Series.
PR6013.R367Z65   1982   828'.809   82-8417
ISBN 0-8057-6839-4   AACR2

Contents

About the Author

G. A. Cevasco, an associate professor of English at St. John's University, New York, completed his undergraduate study at St. John's, his graduate study at Columbia University. A Fellow of the Royal Society of Arts, his publications include nine books, dozens of scholarly articles, and over three hundred book reviews. Most of his work has appeared in American journals, but he has also been published in England, Ireland, Canada, Italy, France, Taiwan, and the Philippines. In addition to serving as a literary critic for several publications, he continually delves into material related to his own special field of study, Aestheticism and Decadence in British literature, 1870–1900. His previous book, *J.-K. Huysmans: A Reference Guide* (G. K. Hall, 1980), covers the influence that the author of *A Rebours* had on the Decadence, considers the part he played in Naturalism and Impressionism, and traces his influence upon such figures as George Moore, Oscar Wilde, Max Beerbohm, Aubrey Beardsley, and John Gray.

Preface

Virtually all the figures in the so-called English Decadence burned themselves out at an early age, took to alcohol or drugs, committed suicide, or died in disgrace. Their lives have received the same attention so frequently accorded the nineties. One writer of the period who does not fit the stereotype, whose life has not been spotlighted, is John Gray. His long and productive life, however, has recently begun to attract the attention of literary historians, critics, and scholars. His works, which have never been popular, are beginning to reach a wider circle of readers.

Interest in Gray has been slowly building. Indeed, it is only now, almost fifty years after his death, that all of his poetry is being prepared for publication, that his letters are being collected, that his place in the nineties is being fully questioned.

To what degree, for example, did John Gray foster Decadent trends? What direct and indirect contributions did he make to the literature of his age? What specifically was his relationship with Oscar Wilde, Aubrey Beardsley, Ernest Dowson, Lionel Johnson, William Butler Yeats, and André Raffalovich? If he were not the prototype of Wilde's Dorian Gray, why did Wilde and others refer to Gray as "Dorian"? And why did Wilde allude to Gray in *De Profundis* as he did? What caused the break between the two?

John Gray moved far beyond the role of a Dorian Gray. At the time of his death in 1934, he had won respect as a priest, a poet, and an essayist. An individual whose tastes were always exact and exquisite, Canon Gray's interests ranged from theology to ethnology, from Japanese artifacts to music and toys. As a committed man of letters, his facility with words never failed him. As a poet, he wrote distinctive, introspective verse.

Gray was so autobiographical a writer, in fact, that to know the genesis, the evolution, the composition of his poetry, plays, essays, and fiction is to begin to understand him, to appreciate why he wrote what he did in the way that he did. This study, however, does not aim at inclusive biography; the basic facts, events, vicissitudes of Gray's life are discussed only insofar as they help to deal with the direct and indirect contributions he made to the literature of his age.

Beyond the first chapter, biography plays mainly a supportive role. The five chapters that follow attempt to bring Gray the man of letters into focus. All that he wrote is unfolded from its humble beginnings through the early productions of his plays to the publication of his poetry, essays, and fiction. The approach to his major works is analytical and critical, to his other, lesser, literary activities, mainly descriptive. A concluding chapter evaluates Gray the poet, the playwright, the fiction writer, the essayist and assesses his reputation.

My reliance upon the small company of Gray scholars must be noted. The extent of my indebtedness can be read from my notes and bibliography, but a special debt to Brocard Sewell, O. Carm., needs to be acknowledged. Two of his books, *Two Friends: John Gray & André Raffalovich* (1963) and *Footnote to the Nineties* (1968), initiated the current, though still somewhat limited, interest in Gray, and I am most appreciative for the help and encouragement he has given me. The photograph of John Gray opposite the title page was supplied through the kindness of Dr. Paul Winckler of Long Island University, C. W. Post Center, Greenvale, New York.

Although my study may not greatly alter Gray's reputation, it should throw additional light upon his literary career. If my efforts provide a sound, up-to-date, and readable evaluation of the poetry and prose of John Gray, it will have achieved its primary purpose.

G. A. Cevasco

St. John's University

Chronology

1866 John Gray born March 10 at Woolwich, London.

1872 Enters Mr. Nichols' Wesleyan Day School.

1878 Awarded a scholarship to the Roan Grammar School. Wins an essay contest sponsored by the Royal Humane Society on the subject of cruelty to animals. Passes examination for entrance to Woolwich Arsenal for the Trades.

1879 Modest family financial circumstances force him to leave school. At Arsenal, becomes a proficient metal-turner.

1884 Passes competitive examination for a Lower Division Clerkship. Appointed to the General Post Office.

1888 Transferred to the Foreign Office, where he works as a librarian.

1889 First publications in the *Dial*, essays, poetry, and fiction. Probable first meeting with Oscar Wilde.

1890 Takes instructions in the doctrines of the Roman Church; formally received on March 10.

1891 Frequent guest with Wilde at the Rhymers' Club; here meets Lionel Johnson, Ernest Dowson, William Butler Yeats, Arthur Symons, and other club members. To them, he is affectionately known as "Dorian Gray."

1892 Begins writing "The Person in Question," a story of dislocation reminiscent of *The Picture of Dorian Gray*. Meets André Raffalovich and, through him, Verlaine, Mallarmé, Marcel Schwob, and other French Symbolists. Lectures on "The Modern Actor" at the Playgoer's Club; Wilde in the

Chair. Begins libel action against *The Star* for identifying him as the prototype of Dorian Gray.

1893   The Bodley Head publishes his first volume of poetry, *Silverpoints*.

1894   Completes his first drama, *Sour Grapes*, a one-act play. Collaborates with Raffalovich on a play, *The Blackmailers*; presented at the Prince of Wales Theatre, June 17. With Raffalovich, writes two short duologues, *A Northern Aspect* and *The Ambush of Young Days*. Undergoes a second and lasting spiritual conversion. Distributes his first *Blue Calendar*.

1895   Sends barrister to Wilde trials in case his name should be introduced. Second *Blue Calendar*.

1896   Publishes *Spiritual Poems*. Third *Blue Calendar*.

1897   Final *Blue Calendar*.

1898   Leaves for Rome to qualify for Roman Catholic priesthood. Registers in The Scots College.

1901   Ordained to the priesthood on December 21.

1902   Takes up his first clerical appointment as curate at St. Patrick's Church, Edinburgh.

1904   Edits and publishes *Last Letters of Aubrey Beardsley*.

1907   Appointed rector of St. Peter's, Edinburgh, a uniquely beautiful church built through the lavish generosity of Raffalovich.

1923   Weekly guest at social functions hosted by Raffalovich at his Edinburgh "salons"; among many celebrities are Henry James, Arthur Symons, Eric Gill, Max Beerbohm, Hilaire Belloc, Gordon Bottomly, and Compton Mackenzie.

1926   Publishes *The Long Road*. Allows publication of "The Song of the Stars" and "Sound," two poems excluded from *Silverpoints* (1893).

1928   Begins contributing essays and poetry to *Blackfriars*.

1930 Named canon of the diocese of St. Andrews and Edinburgh.

1931 Publishes *Poems*. Writes first installment of *Park*, a novella.

1932 Writes second, third, and fourth installments of *Park*. Publishes *Park: A Fantastic Story*.

1934 Last published article: an obituary in *Blackfriars* for his lifelong companion, André Raffalovich. Four months after the death of Raffalovich, Gray dies on June 16. Pontifical Mass of Requiem celebrated in St. Peter's Church, Edinburgh.

Chapter One

The Subject
An Unfamiliar Figure

John Gray is a somewhat unfamiliar figure in modern literature. Some readers associate him only with an evocative volume of poems, *Silverpoints*. Others may recall that he was a member of the Wilde circle, that he is mentioned in *De Profundis* when Wilde bewails that he should have remained on friendly terms with Gray instead of taking up with Lord Alfred Douglas.

Better informed readers know that nothing of any substance was published about Gray until 1961.[1] After his death in 1934, his family and friends preferred to keep his name out of the public eye. His manuscripts and papers were collected and stored in the Dominican Chaplaincy, Edinburgh. The Dominicans were well aware of Gray's literary accomplishments, but they did not want his later years as a dedicated priest sullied in any way with undue emphasis on his early days as Decadent and dandy,[2] especially since some forty years before, he had been connected by scandal with Wilde. In 1895, at the time of Wilde's folly and public humiliation, Gray had instructed a competent attorney to attend the trials with a watching brief on his behalf in case his name were mentioned. It was not.

A few years before, however, Gray had been prominently referred to in the press as one of Wilde's protégés. He had also been supposedly identified as the real-life hero of *The Picture of Dorian Gray*. The Wilde-Gray relationship is complicated and difficult to trace, but a rupture in their friendship had already occurred when

Wilde stood trial. Gray seems not to have offered his support and kept discreetly away; but, then, virtually all of Wilde's friends and associates also remained at a safe distance.

Through Wilde, Gray had met many of the celebrities of the period. He became acquainted with Aubrey Beardsley,[3] Ernest Dowson, Lionel Johnson, Arthur Symons, William Butler Yeats, and many another poet and publisher. Wilde introduced Gray to Ada Leverson and Frank Harris, to John Lane and Elkin Mathews, to various members of the Rhymers' Club. On his own, Gray established relationships with several figures in the Parisian coterie of the 1890s, particularly with Pierre Louÿs and Paul Verlaine. The most significant of all Gray's friendships, one that continued for more than forty years, began when Symons introduced him to André Raffalovich.[4]

From a literary point of view, Gray had much in common with Raffalovich and other young aesthetes of the period. That he differed from them radically in many ways should be emphasized. Unlike Raffalovich, who had wealth and social standing, Gray came from a poor working-class family. Unlike Beardsley, who passed away in his twenty-sixth year, Gray declined to die young and lived into his late sixties. Unlike Dowson and Johnson, who dissipated their lives away with alcohol and also died quite young, Gray, after a period of confusion and depression, determined upon a positive response to life. Like Wilde, Raffalovich, Beardsley, Dowson, and Johnson, he converted to the Church of Rome.

Gray's conversion was so deep and lasting that he decided to prepare for the priesthood. On December 21, 1901, after completing his theological studies at The Scots College, Rome, he was ordained a Roman Catholic priest by Cardinal Respighi in the Basilica of St. John Lateran. Following his ordination, Father Gray spent four months in Rome and three more in Fribourg.

His first clerical assignment took him to Edinburgh. Here in the Cowgate section of the city, he labored at St. Patrick's Church among the mostly Irish families who, a few decades before, had flocked to Scotland in search of work. Indications are that Gray served his flock well. Known as a priest who would offer his help to anyone in need, he was welcomed into every home throughout his parish.

The everyday routine of a curate and dedicated community servant did not allow Gray much time for writing; still, he never abandoned literature entirely. For several years after his ordination, he wrote only a few hymns and devotional verses. During the last decades of his life, however, he once more gave free rein to his creativity. In his sixtieth year, he wrote: "I see more beauty in the world as I grow older. I hope to write less and better with time."[5] But he still managed to compose two more volumes of poetry, many essays, and a short novel.

From his earliest days as a writer, Gray had always been fastidious, a conscientious poet in pursuit of the beautiful. When he wrote, it was mainly because of an aesthetic drive to satisfy himself and bring a bit of pleasure to those who might be responsive to his art. If his poetry brought him social acceptance and limited fame, that would be fine. Dreams of great wealth or popular appeal, however, never crossed his mind—and this is unusual in one who came from such a humble, lower-middle-class background as did John Gray.

Birth and Early Days

John Henry Gray was born on March 10, 1866, at Number Two, Vivian Road, Bethnal Green, London. His father, after whom he was named, was a journeyman carpenter. His mother, Hannah Mary Williamson, after her marriage, like most women of the period, took up the duties of housewife and mainstay of the home. Over the next twenty-one years, eight more children, four sons and four daughters, were born to John and Hannah Gray.

Though John Gray, Sr., did not earn much as a carpenter and wheelwright in the Woolwich Dockyard, he provided sufficiently for his wife and children; and, like most hardworking family men, he always held onto hopes for a better future. Concerned about the future of his first-born son, he and his wife, being Nonconformists, decided that John Henry should be educated at Mr. Nichols' Wesleyan Day School on Plumstead Common Road.

Their son proved to be an alert and able student, eager to learn all that his schoolmasters could offer his young mind. When he was twelve, he was awarded a scholarship to the Roan Grammar School at Maze Hill, Blackheath. At Roan, he was regarded as a conscientious student of gentle disposition, one with a gift for words. That he was highly articulate and mentally superior to most of his classmates can be inferred from an essay he wrote on the subject "Cruelty to Animals." His essay was singled out for a prize by the Royal Humane Society, a distinction that allowed him, his parents, and his schoolmasters a measure of pride.

Although well pleased with their son's academic performance, John and Hannah Gray nonetheless had to withdraw him from Roan when he was fifteen. Modest circumstances made it imperative that their eldest son contribute to the support of his younger brothers and sisters. There was little that his schoolmasters could do about his early withdrawal other than note on his records that his character and conduct had been excellent.

He entered the Woolwich Arsenal. Within a short time, he became a skilled metal-turner, and he applied himself to his trade as conscientiously as he had applied himself to his school work. In his leisure, he continued with his studies. His aptitude for learning made it possible for him to master Latin, French, and German. Interested in art and music, he learned to play the violin and taught himself to draw and paint. That young John Gray was destined to be more than a metal-turner became apparent to all. Encouraged by his supervisors, he took a promotional examination. An excellent grade on the test earned him a place in the drawing office of the Arsenal.

Working at the Arsenal had meager rewards, so young Gray, eager for further challenges, began to study for the entrance examinations of the Civil Service. In his eighteenth year, he passed a competitive examination for a Lower Division Clerkship. On December 20, 1884, he received an appointment to the General Post

Office. Four years later, on November 16, 1888, he was promoted to the position of librarian in the Foreign Office.

With his career in Civil Service assured, Gray could now turn to what had become his chief interest—literature. When he first gave serious thought to becoming a writer, and what nurtured his aspirations, cannot be determined. What is known is that he had begun the writing of poetry early in his teens. Little of his earliest efforts survive. The manuscript of one extant poem, however, demonstrates quite clearly that Gray had more than just a facility with words. Inscribed "Writ by me when I was sixteen years old," this poem must have convinced its young author that he could succeed as a writer.[6]

The hours Gray spent at his desk in the Foreign Office were long but not demanding. He directed most of his energy into his vocation of being creative with words. And so he experimented with hundreds of poems, wrote dozens of essays, and tried his skill at translating French and German works. Some day, he knew, he would find recognition as a writer.

Among the Literati

When not practicing his craft, Gray mixed in the literary life of London, attended as many first nights as he could, and spent long hours in music halls. He haunted all the places where young writers were known to assemble. Night after night he could be seen at the Café Royal, or the Florence Restaurant, or the Crown in Charing Cross Road. His favorite spot was the Cheshire Cheese, where the Rhymers' Club held most of its meetings.

At the Rhymers' Gray enjoyed many an evening in the company of Oscar Wilde, Lionel Johnson, Ernest Dowson, Arthur Symons, William Butler Yeats, and other aesthetes who, if they were not reading their poems to one another, were fervently discussing aspects of poetry and life. Although much attached to all the talented members of the club and very much a permanent guest, Gray, like Wilde, was not an official member. But he could boast of membership in the Playgoers' Club, an elite group of writers and critics with an expressed interest in drama. A lecture he gave there on February 7, 1892, created a flurry of excitement.

An invitation to address the Playgoers' was quite an honor, and Gray had been singled out to do so because he had established himself as a young man of sensitive tastes, an individual with an abiding interest in the theater. He decided to speak on "The Modern Actor."[7] What he had to say was more critical than complimentary. "Mr. John Gray," wrote a critic who covered the lecture for the *Daily Telegraph*, "has builded himself a world of strange feerie, wherein he dwells, anticipating the re-birth of the native drama within its limits. His view is that of the artistic pagan, and is vaporously expressed." In flippant fashion, the critic questioned Gray's censorious approach to his subject. He also described Gray's diction as "irridescent, or perhaps scented." As for Gray's delivery, it was "gentle"; and when Gray came to the end of his talk, "he ceased: he did not conclude."[8]

The fact that Wilde moderated the meeting at which Gray spoke inclined the critic to link the two. In his report on Gray's lecture, he referred to the speaker as a "protégé" of Wilde's. Whatever the connotations the term "protégé" was meant to carry, Gray was not pleased. Accordingly, Wilde wrote a letter of protest, which the *Telegraph* published. All artists in this vulgar age, Wilde began, could use protection; but Gray, who had delivered "the brilliant fantastic lecture on 'The Modern Actor,'" had such "a high indifference of temper," took such pleasure "in the creation of beautiful things and the long contemplation of them," and disdained "what in life is common and ignoble," was not in need of another's protection, "nor would he accept it."[9]

John "Dorian" Gray

Gray and Wilde would have ignored the "protégé" remark of the *Telegraph* critic except that the press had linked their names just two weeks before. On the front page of its February 6, 1892, issue, the *Star* discussed their relationship. In a popular column, "Mainly about People," Gray was described as a young man "who has cultivated his manner to the highest pitch of languor yet attained," a dandy who was a well-known figure at the Playgoers' Club, "where, though he often speaks, is seldom heard." Ordinarily Gray would have smiled at such a witticism, forced though it was, but he decided not to ignore the column's identification of him as "the original Dorian of the same name."[10]

It was hardly a secret, as the writer for the *Star* well knew, that several members of the Rhymers' Club usually greeted Gray, not as John, but as Dorian. Lionel Johnson recorded the identification in a letter. "I have just made great friends with the original of Dorian," he wrote, "a youth...aged thirty, with the face of fifteen."[11] Dowson, already a friend, wrote in one of his letters that one night at the Rhymers' Club "Dorian Gray [read] some very beautiful and obscure versicles in the latest manner of French Symbolism."[12] William Rothenstein in one of his letters remarked that one day he saw Dorian Gray wandering about Chelsea under the name of John Gray.[13]

There is no reason to infer that Gray took offense—not at first, anyway—at the wide use of his affectionate nickname. In a letter he sent Wilde, dated January 9, 1891, he even closed with the words "Yours ever, Dorian."[14] Almost every account of Gray's movements between 1891 and 1893 alludes to him as "Dorian" Gray. Why, then, the question arises, did he object to the *Star's* identification of him as "the original Dorian of the same name"?

Part of the answer hinges on the fact that shortly after Wilde met Lord Alfred Douglas in 1891, they entered into a scandalous liaison. For Gray to be named publicly as one of Wilde's protégés or as the original of Dorian Gray was to recommend that Gray, like Douglas, was one of Wilde's intimates. Exactly what relationship existed between Wilde and Gray cannot be established, but the sexual side of their relationship was probably more sentimental than lustful. By the spring or early summer of 1892, however, Gray had become part of a homosexual clique which numbered among its members such diverse figures as Wilde, the French poet Pierre Louÿs, and Edward Shelley, an office boy at the Bodley Head publishing house.

The question of Gray's homosexuality remains open to speculation. Admittedly, he could have had a homosexual history, but there is nothing to support such a contention. If not homoerotic early in the nineties, he actively associated with several individuals who were; still, there is no direct evidence.[15] As for the close relationship that developed between Gray and Raffalovich, it could have been less than Platonic at first. Later, it would seem, their attachment was dignified, chaste, and dedicated to spiritual ends. Whatever the facts may be, Gray came to accept a dichotomy about homosexuality that Raffalovich established.

Raffalovich, who had a homosexual nature, maintained that there are two distinct types of sexual inverts. The "inferior" type simply craves venereal pleasure. The "superior" type sublimates his venereal appetite in order to enhance the intellectual and spiritual side of man.[16] The relationship between Gray and Raffalovich, their correspondence indicates, was of a "superior" nature.

Fearful that Gray's affection for Wilde might be, or might become, something less than ideal, Raffalovich cautioned Gray that for him to continue camaraderie with the author of *The Picture of Dorian Gray* was unwise. An element of jealousy may have initially motivated Raffalovich, but apparently he was seriously concerned about Gray. And yet Gray may have at first ignored Raffalovich's admonition; for Raffalovich finally gave Gray what amounted to an ultimatum: "You cannot be Oscar's friend and mine."[17] Reason prevailed over emotion and Gray slowly inclined toward Raffalovich.

It soon became obvious to Gray that for him to continue an association with Wilde was to live, like the fictional Dorian Gray, in an underworld fraught with danger. For the *Star* to label John Gray the original of Dorian Gray made the young author aware of what such a designation implied and of what might follow; accordingly, he initiated proceedings for libel. The *Star*, cognizant of the implications of its charge, preferred to evade legal action. A retraction was agreed upon.

"We are told that some people have taken quite seriously a suggestion ... that Mr. Gray was the prototype of Oscar Wilde's

Dorian Gray," the *Star* subsequently noted. "The risks of the New Humour could not have a more unfortunate illustration than the acceptance as serious of a statement that a skilled young literary artist of promise like Mr. Gray could possibly be the original of the monstrous Epicurean of Mr. Wilde's creation, and we greatly regret the erroneous impression that has been produced."[18]

In case Wilde might also have been ruffled by the *Star's* original statement, the identifying of John Gray as the original of Dorian Gray, its editors considered it wise to pacify him, too. "Apart from the fact that Mr. Wilde's acquaintance with Mr. Gray did not commence until after the publication of this novel," the recantation continued, "Mr. Wilde would be as likely to draw a character from life as to call a photograph an artistic production. Character sketching he regards as literary work, but not as literary art."[19]

The fact is that Wilde occasionally put real-life acquaintances into his fiction.[20] Why, though, did the *Star* claim that Wilde and Gray did not meet until after the publication of *Dorian Gray*? There are several good reasons for believing that Gray and Wilde had met as early as 1889.

Before being published in an expanded version in April 1891, *The Picture of Dorian Gray* had appeared in the July 1890 issue of *Lippincott's Monthly Magazine*. This means that if Wilde knew John Gray before or during the period he wrote his novel, they would have had to meet in 1890, or even before. Exactly when and where Gray and Wilde first met cannot be established.

There is nothing to substantiate the conjecture that Gray, in 1889, "was picked up by Oscar Wilde . . . in a bar near Shaftsbury Avenue."[21] The year of their meeting seems right, however; for, as a more reasonable supposition has it, Gray and Wilde "probably first encountered each other at the house rented by the artists Charles Ricketts and Charles Shannon at No. 1, The Vale."[22]

In August of 1889, Ricketts and Shannon sent Wilde a gift issue of their first publication, the *Dial*, to which Gray had contributed a perceptive essay, "Les Goncourts," and a beautifully crafted short story, "The Great Worm." Shortly thereafter, Wilde stopped by The Vale to thank Ricketts and Shannon for their sending him a copy of their new periodical. Finding the two young artists "very cultivated and interesting,"[23] he soon became a frequent visitor. On one of his visits Wilde probably was introduced to Gray, one of the chief contributors to the first and subsequent issues of the *Dial*.

Even if Wilde had begun the writing of *Dorian Gray* as early as 1888, as has been suggested,[24] he must have been still working on it in 1889 when, as it seems likely, he met Gray. Is it just co-incidental, therefore, that at the beginning of Wilde's novel, Dorian is young, outstandingly good-looking, and relatively untouched, as was John Gray when Wilde first met him; and that changes wrought in Dorian come about chiefly under the influence of an older man, Lord Henry Wotton, a sybarite reminiscent of Wilde himself?

A comparison of the two versions of *Dorian Gray*, the pre-liminary version of July 1890 and the expanded version of April 1891, furthermore, reveals much about Wilde's developing thought and style. Not only do his revisions show how he improved the action, the balance of the novel, as well as details of style, but the revisions tantalize a reader of both versions to speculate upon what part Wilde's meeting with John Gray may have had upon *The Picture of Dorian Gray*.

Did Wilde, for example, initially call his protagonist "Dorian Gray"? Could the name of his hero have been altered after he met John Gray? Did Wilde etch in so many of the details that seem to recommend John Gray as a prototype of Dorian Gray after the two had actually met?

To what extent the real John Gray may have been transfigured into the fictional Dorian Gray is one of those questions, like that of Gray's homosexuality in the nineties, that cannot be completely resolved. It would seem to be more than simple coincidence, how-ever, that shortly after the *Star* published its retraction, Gray began writing "The Person in Question," a short story that reflects his restlessness, his dissatisfaction with the Dorian Gray kind of life he had been leading. He completed the work, but did not publish it. To have done so would have revealed too much. The fact that Gray did not destroy the manuscript, that he stored "The Person in Question" among his private papers, allows the inference that he thought highly of this autobiographical bit of fiction, that he planned to publish the work someday.

When "The Person in Question" was finally published, twenty-four years after Gray's death and almost seventy years after it had been written, once again it provoked speculation on that fascinating question: Was John Gray, as the *Star* had originally charged in 1892, the original of Dorian Gray?

A Writer of Promise

In its retraction, the *Star* hoped to appease Gray as much as possible and so referred to him as "a skillful young artist of promise." The words were more than simple flattery, for Gray had published an essay, a short story, and poetry in the *Dial*, and he had also done quite a bit of translating. True, he had not produced anything substantial; but, as the *Star* had conceded, Gray did show promise.

More than likely, the writer of the retraction for the *Star* had not read Gray's early publications. Gray was pleased, nonetheless, that he had evoked such adulation. And like every neophyte author, Gray was pleased with his initial appearances in print.

Two of his first efforts, "Les Goncourts," an enthusiastic essay on the merits of the Goncourt brothers, and "The Great Worm," a short story, had both appeared in the first issue of the *Dial*, a literary journal of some merit that began publication in 1889. Three years later, the *Dial* published "Parsifal," "Heart's Demesne," and "Les Desmoiselles de Sauve"—three poems that Gray later included in his remarkable volume of poetry, *Silverpoints*. Also in 1892, Gray collaborated with A. Teixeira de Mattos in translating *Ecstasy, A Study of Happiness*, a work of the Dutch novelist Louis Couperus.

An excellent translation of Theodore de Banville's "Le Baiser" into rhymed couplets that Gray completed in the same year brought him a measure of added attention. This delightful one-act play, one of the better efforts of the minor French playwright, was produced at the Royalty Theatre on the evening of March 6. Once again, the *Star* fawned over Gray. "Mr. John Gray," its drama critic effused, "has been wonderfully successful in Englishing the dainty, delicate, tripping verse of Banville, and the rhymes are a delight to the ear."[25] The *Star* also reported that J. M. Barrie and Henry James were present in the stalls; George Moore and Oscar Wilde, in private boxes. Most newsworthy, perhaps, was the fact that Wilde and his young gentlemen companions were all wearing green carnations.

In 1892, Gray also translated four short stories of P. C. J. Bourget, which were published under the title *A Saint and Others*. Next, he wrote a prefatory note for what purported to be a translation from the Italian of a work written by an Emilio Montanaro. The translator, J. T. Grein, however, had written the work himself. An anonymous critic for the *Star* carped that Grein's spoof was "the latest fleur du mal," and he wrote rather slightingly of Gray's introduction.[26]

Toward the end of the same year, Gray met André Raffalovich, an aristocratic Parisian Jew from a prominent banking family. Arthur Symons introduced them at a gathering of writers and dandies. Raffalovich, who liked to consider himself a patron of the arts, offered Gray the kind of encouragement a young author likes to hear. Gray, for his part, was impressed with Raffalovich's warmth, his polished manners, his intellectual attainments. Their chance meeting flowered into a rare relationship.

Gray soon learned that shortly before Raffalovich had been born, his family, to escape religious coercion, fled Russia and migrated to France. When it was decreed that all Jews in Russia must either join the Orthodox Church or leave the country, Herman and Marie Raffalovich, André's parents, chose exile. For economic reasons they settled in Paris, where Herman prospered and soon became a banker of international repute. His wife, a woman of impressive beauty and creative intelligence, became hostess to fashionable men and women of Parisian society; her salons were frequented by prominent artists and writers, financiers and scientists, professors and politicians.

André, the youngest of the Raffalovichs' three children, possessed his father's financial acumen, but he had no desire to enter the banking business. In 1882, when he was in his eighteenth year, he decided to study at Oxford University. He traveled to England, met with Walter Pater, and arranged to matriculate at Balliol College. Poor health forced him to delay his plans. Instead of entering Oxford, he decided to take up residence in a fashionable section of London.

Early in the nineties, having ample means, André Raffalovich began to entertain on a lavish scale. Most of his guests and acquaintances liked him, considered him urbane and talented; a few thought him a bit affected and too much the dilettante. His mother was well known in Paris for her successful salons; he hoped for the same in London. And in addition to playing host at his many soirées, he contributed to French literary reviews and wrote poetry. By the time he and Gray met in 1892, Raffalovich had published several critical essays, four volumes of verse, and a novel.

There was never any rivalry between Gray and Raffalovich, but it was apparent to both that all that Gray had written up to this time was of an experimental nature. Most of his efforts had been ignored or slighted, and only a few pieces had received a word or two of praise. But in the following year, 1893, Gray fulfilled his promise with *Silverpoints*. This remarkable volume, which became one of the most famous books of the nineties, introduced contemporary French poetry to the British public. During this same *annus mirabilis*, he contributed five short stories to the *Butterfly*, a well-received but short-lived literary periodical, translated a hymn from the Italian of St. Francis of Assisi for the *Dial*, and wrote an essay on Garth Wilkinson's *Improvisation from the Spirit*, also for the *Dial*.

In the spring of the following year, Gray concerned himself mainly with the craft of playwriting. On April 17, 1894, his masque *Sour Grapes*, with music by F. Gilbert and C. Dick, was presented at the West Theatre, Albert Hall. Two months later, on June 17, *The Blackmailers*, a joint effort of Gray and Raffalovich, was performed at the Prince of Wales Theatre. They went on to write two more short plays, *A Northern Aspect* and *The Ambush of Young Days.*

If Gray did not receive accolades for his dramatic works, he could be assured by the attention he began to receive as a poet. The favorable reception accorded *Silverpoints* convinced Gray that he would do well to concentrate on verse. Several poems that he wrote during 1896 were accordingly directed to the *Dial*, the *Savoy*, and the *Pageant*. The most important work that Gray completed at this period in his life, however, was his *Spiritual Poems.* As its title indicates, this volume was made up of religious poetry. Internal evidence allows the inference that several of these spiritual poems had been composed about the same time as his *Silverpoints*, but the publication of *Spiritual Poems* in 1896 signaled a change in the direction of Gray's life.

This change became evident to his close friends. After reading through *Spiritual Poems*, Dowson, for example, was moved to write Symons that Gray had found a new interest. "John Gray has sent me his new book...," he wrote. "I cannot determine whether his mysticism is sincere or merely a pose—but I think it is the former."[27] Had Dowson or Symons read an article that Gray had contributed to the *Dial* about the same time as his *Spiritual Poems* was published, they would have been aware that their friend was inclining more and more toward the mystical. That article was "The Redemption of Durtal," a discussion of *Là-Bas* and *En Route*, two novels of J.-K. Huysmans in which Gray discussed the conversion of the French novelist to Catholicism and Huysmans's fascination with things of the spirit.

A Spiritual Quest

Gray, like Huysmans, had been drawn to Catholicism. The French author arrived at the threshold of faith after a prolonged period of depression, after developing an interest in liturgical art, and after, as is obvious from the diabolism in *Là-Bas*, he came to accept a principle of evil. If Satan exists, Huysmans concluded, then God must exist. Gray's conversion, however, was neither as extreme nor as dramatic as Huysmans's.

In 1889, at a time when Gray was troubled by the aimless drift of his life and anxious about his future, he was invited by a friend, Marmaduke Langdale, to spend the summer with him and his family at the Breton fishing village of St. Quay-Portrieux. The Langdales were a close-knit Catholic family. Their staunch faith and the simple faith of the Bretons made a deep impression upon Gray. And here in Brittany his conversion took place. The experiences of this holiday were such that Gray referred to them as "stars in the sky of my memory."[28]

Upon his return to England, he took instructions in the doctrines of the church. Several months later, on March 10, 1890, he was formally baptized in London at the Church of Saints Anselm and Cecelia. Shortly thereafter, he was confirmed at St. Mary's Church, Cadogan Gardens, by Dr. James Laird Patterson, titular bishop of Emmaeus and auxiliary bishop to Cardinal Manning.

At the same time that Gray was taking instructions in his adopted faith, Wilde was working on his *Picture of Dorian Gray*. Could Wilde have had John Gray specifically in mind when he wrote that "it was rumored of [Dorian] ... that he was about to join the Roman Catholic communion; and certainly the Roman ritual ... had a great attraction for him"?[29] If so, Wilde knew John Gray better than John Gray knew himself; for Wilde also wrote in his novel that Dorian had "a special passion ... for everything connected with the service of the Church,"[30] but that "mysticism, with its marvellous power of making things strange to us ..., moved him [only] for a season."[31]

Gray's conversion did not endure. Despite his baptism and confirmation, he continued to lead a mundane and meaningless life. He refused to adhere to the moral strictures of his faith. Whether it was weakness or indifference he probably did not realize fully at the time. Not until nine years later, after a great deal of soul-searching, did he make a significant observation. "I went through instructions as blindly and indifferently as ever anyone did," he lamented, "and immediately I began a course of sin compared with which my previous life was innocence."[32]

In *Dorian Gray*, Wilde wrote that his title character "knew that the senses, no less than the soul, have their spiritual mysteries to reveal."[33] And it was to the senses, not to the spirit, that John Gray, as disciple to Wilde, began to devote himself. A modest civil servant during the day, at night he became the dandy, the Decadent. He spent his evenings strolling gas-lit streets and visiting restaurants, pubs, theaters, and the music halls of central London. Dowson summed up the Gray of this period best when he wrote of his friend as being "incurably given over to social things."[34]

Wilde liked to refer to Gray as *the* poet, and Gray played the role in earnest. His verse was as fastidious as his dress. He loved to recite his latest poems at literary salons, and he did so in a gentle, affecting voice. That he read extremely well was remarked upon by Symons. In a letter to Raffalovich, he remarked how Gray won Walter Pater's admiration and friendship after the latter heard the former recite one of his poems. "A certain expression passed over Pater's face," Symons noted, "and he asked Gray to say it over again. 'The rest is silence.' "[35]

Pater, it is claimed, manifested a mild paternal interest in Gray, and when *Silverpoints* appeared, he was one of the first to praise the volume highly.[36] Not only did Gray have Pater's enthusiastic appraisal, but encomiums flowed in from all sides. Gray was accorded all the critical recognition any aspiring poet could hope for; yet he was troubled, so troubled that he apparently even contemplated suicide.[37]

Why Gray fell away from the initial fervor of his attraction to Catholicism he never did say; but what is more significant, he underwent a second conversion a few years later. Toward the end of 1894 or early in 1895, at about the same time that he broke with Wilde, Gray, empty and desperate, once more turned to things of the spirit.

William Muir, one of the few individuals to whom Gray ever spoke about intimate spiritual matters, several years after Gray's death related an incident that sheds light on the resolve of the young poet to amend his life. One morning, it seems, when Gray was walking in the vicinity of Leicester Square, an unidentified individual approached him with some devastating news. Gray strolled on, concerned and confused. Finding himself in front of a Catholic church, he entered to seek a few moments of solace. The next thing he remembered was an old woman bearing keys coming up to him. In a low voice, she told him that she had to lock up the church, that he would have to leave. As Gray began to comply with her request, he was suddenly struck by the darkness. Only then did he realize that he had been on his knees in prayer most of the day. Could the disturbing information imparted by the un-identified individual have been the arrest of Wilde?[38]

At one time, Gray had been proud to be seen with Wilde. He had found an extraordinary stimulus in Wilde's talk, and not being a university man, Gray at first looked up to Wilde as someone who could impart to him the education that a young poet required. Within a short period, their relationship grew intense and idealized, very much like that of Lord Wotton and Dorian Gray. But when Douglas came upon the scene, Gray reacted negatively to Wilde and Bosie's intimacy, their matrimonial exhibitionism.

Wilde, furthermore, was growing fat and foolish. The more he achieved success with such plays as *Lady Windermere's Fan* and *The Importance of Being Earnest*, the more he began to take up with stable boys and assorted roughs. Troubled by the transformation Wilde had undergone, Gray grew fearful that he might end up as his mentor and friend had. Wilde's former disciple determined to turn his life around. This time he would remain steadfast in his spiritual quest.

There is no way to pinpoint the date that Gray first determined to seek the priesthood. The thought could have germinated over several years, or it could have come to him suddenly in 1898 with the death of Aubrey Beardsley. Gray had been instrumental in Beardsley's conversion to Catholicism, and when the controversial artist died at the early age of twenty-six, Gray once more experienced a religious crisis. Again he was forced to reflect upon the direction of his own life. God, he came to conclude, was calling him to something higher than an indulgent life of social posturing and aesthetic experimentation.

Toward the end of 1898, accordingly, he resigned his position in the Foreign Office and made a radical break with the London literary scene. On October 25, he entered The Scots College, Rome, a candidate for holy orders. Though now in his early thirties, he nonetheless quickly settled into the life of a student. From all reports, he got on well with the other seminarians, most of whom were at least ten years younger than he. They were different from his former artist and literary friends, but they accepted Gray as readily as he adjusted to them.

In time, Gray came to love everything about the *Collegio Scozzese*, especially its order and regularity. The years he spent there went by quickly. When he left Rome in 1902, an ordained priest, he was determined to persevere in his vocation. That he did so for the remaining thirty-four years of his life is the best indication of how thoroughly he atoned for any and all indiscretions of his former life as dandy and Decadent.

Gray's first years years as a priest in Edinburgh, working among the poor, visiting them in their dilapidated tenements, must have been trying indeed. But when he first accepted his post at St. Patrick's, he had no delusions about his parish work. Despite his outward aloofness, his ascetic reserve, the sick and the needy knew they could always count on his love and ministration. His zeal became apparent to all.

The writer Moray McLaren, commenting on this period of Gray's life, wrote: "This one-time man of fashion became noted as the priest who would go anywhere, do anything for anyone, and would be welcomed everywhere. It should be remembered that in those days before Cowgate was cleaned up even the sturdiest policemen had to go about in pairs. Fr. Gray had no need of a protective companion. And the later the hour and the dirtier the night, the more gladly he went on his errands of mercy and devotion."[39]

A few years later, through the lavish generosity of Raffalovich,

Gray was able to build a magnificent church, St. Peter the Apostle, in the Morningside section of Edinburgh. On April 25, 1907, the archbishop blessed this uniquely beautiful edifice and installed Gray as rector. Twenty-three years later, Gray was singled out for ecclesiastical distinction when he was named canon of the Diocese of St. Andrews and Edinburgh. He had not labored among his flock for any special recognition, but to have been honored with the title of canon was a tribute to his years of diligence as a parish priest and an outward sign of the esteem in which he was held by the Scottish hierarchy.

Canon Gray had traveled a long way along his own private road to Damascus.

In Edinburgh

Apart from vacations that took him to the Continent, England, Wales, and Iceland, Gray spent the rest of his life in Edinburgh. In becoming a priest, he thought that he might have to abandon his literary activities, and for some twenty years after his ordination, he wrote little more than a few hymns and devotional verses. That he was primarily concerned with the worship of God and service to his fellowman was obvious to all who knew him. A dedicated man of the cloth, he was still—under the cloth—a man of letters. One day he even confided to a priest friend: "I would be a saint, but I have not the time. I have to keep abreast of modern literature."[40]

In addition to his clerical duties, Gray, shortly after he took up residence in Edinburgh, began to edit some correspondence that he and Raffalovich had had with Aubrey Beardsley. In 1904, he published *The Last Letters of Aubrey Beardsley.* Most of the letters had been addressed to Raffalovich, who had helped support the artist during the last few months of his life, and a few had been sent to Gray himself. Shortly after the artist's death some six years before, Gray had composed a moving tribute, in French, to his late friend that had been published in the May 1, 1898, issue of

La Revue Blanche, a Parisian journal. A proper tribute to Beardsley in English, Gray decided, would be a volume of the artist's last letters. They would best reveal Beardsley's true inner nature.

After the Beardsley book, Gray published nothing for eighteen years. Finally, in 1922, he broke his self-imposed literary silence with *Vivis,* a small volume of poetry that was privately printed in a limited edition of seventy-five copies. Four years later, he published his first major work in almost thirty years, *The Long Road.* This work, an allegory of human life, is interesting for many reasons, one of the chief being its many autobiographical allusions. *The Long Road* includes a revised and re-ordered version of his *Vivis* poems (now entitled *Quatrains*), as well as a rather long poem entitled "The Flying Fish" that had been published thirty years before in the *Dial.*

In 1926, he also translated some prayers from the Latin *Revelations* of Saints Gertrude and Mechtilde, two thirteenth-century nuns of the Abbey of Helfta, near Eisleben. The work was published under the title *O Beata Trinitas.* Indications are that this book of prayers, which is completely devoid of the mawkishness often attendant on translations of this kind, became Gray's own favorite book of devotions. A second edition was issued in 1928 under a new title, *The True Prayers of St. Gertrude and St. Mechtilde.*

During this period of his life, Gray was a weekly guest at the literary salons that Raffalovich hosted at his comfortable home, 9 Whitehouse Terrace, Edinburgh. Shortly after Gray took up his work as curate at St. Patrick's Church, Raffalovich had followed him to Edinburgh. Finding the climate favorable and the city inviting, in the spring of 1905 he purchased Whitehouse Terrace; and then for twenty-seven years, until death was to claim them both, Gray and Raffalovich kept up a close relationship. Like Gray, Raffalovich had also converted to Roman Catholicism, and each morning he attended mass said by Gray at St. Peter's Church.

The greater part of the expense of erecting St. Peter's had been borne by Raffalovich, and when St. Peter's stood completed on April 25, 1907, few of its original parishioners knew that its reserved and dignified pastor had once belonged to a brilliant London circle of writers and artists.

Gray's parishioners appreciated the sanctity of St. Peter's and held their pastor in high esteem. Some of his fellow priests in the diocese of Edinburgh did not know quite how to respond to Father Gray, however. They could not fault his zeal, his piety, but it is understandable that they may have envied him his majestic church and comfortable rectory. Whereas their accommodations were generally sparse, their rooms often cold and damp, they knew that Father Gray lived as sumptuously as a Renaissance bishop.

The presbytery of St. Peter's Church was of set purpose built low and small to accord with the rather humble homes that surround it. Inside the presbytery, a heavy velvet-like fitted carpet made everything upon it seem purposeful and gracious. Stained-glass windows and others leaded with semi-opaque glass enhanced its outer beauty and provided a dim, mysterious twilight within. One visitor to Gray's rectory remarked that it seemed "a world of half-tones."[41] The only thing needed, he remarked further, was the music of Debussy or bits of Maeterlinck to make it quite perfect: "To think of *Pelléas et Mélissanda* or *Le Cathédrale Englouti* is to capture the impression of St. Peter's presbytery—and its creator."[42]

One of the most interesting rooms was Gray's study, which held a tremendous collection of books. One wall not covered floor to ceiling with his books of poetry, art, music, and theology held lithographs by Ricketts and Shannon. Other walls in the presbytery held works of a few prominent Art Nouveau artists. Pieces of sculpture were decoratively placed here and there.

Every night, Gray slept comfortably between black linen sheets. During the day, he presided over a well-ordered household provisioned with a full larder and excellent wines. As for his wardrobe, though most diocesan priests had but two clerical suits, a cassock or two, and a few shirts, Gray's closets bulged with clothing. When he said mass, which involved numerous genuflections, he wore knee breeches so as not to spoil the creases in his trousers, of which he had seven pairs, worn in turn day by day.

While Gray had his priestly duties to perform and parishioners to minister to, Raffalovich enjoyed a sedate life. His chief interests were his friends, his books, and the practice of his religion. In addition, he relished entertaining distinguished visitors to Edinburgh. Virtually every eminent person who visited the city became a guest at Whitehouse Terrace. Celebrities, such as Eric Gill, Gordon Bottomly, Compton Mackenzie, Arthur Symons, Hilaire Belloc, Max Beerbohm, and Henry James, enjoyed the ambiance of Raffalovich's home.

Gray never returned to London, but even with the passage of years, he could hardly forget his friends and acquaintances of the nineties. Occasionally he might refer to them in oblique terms. That he preferred not to discuss Wilde at all became obvious to anyone who might ask him a question about the playwright. "Poor Oscar," Gray would invariably respond, and then abruptly shift to another subject.[43] Now and again he did speak of Dowson and Johnson.

One day, to the amusement of some friends, he related how Dowson frequently scribbled verses on tablecloths in a Soho restaurant where he wooed a young Polish waitress. Another time, Gray even went as far as to describe Dowson's wailing and lamentations when he first learned that the waitress—his Cynara—had eloped with a chef. The waitress had inspired Dowson's memorable line, "I have been faithful to thee, Cynara! in my fashion"; but her unfaithfulness to him, so it was believed, almost broke the poet's heart.[44]

Despite the inherent humor of such an anecdote, Gray was always sympathetic to Dowson, as he was also to Johnson; but humor can often help blot out pain. The one story about Johnson that Gray allowed himself concerned a hubbub one day outside a restaurant door. "Whatever's that?" someone asked. "Only Lionel crying for his perambulator" came back the answer. As everyone knew, Johnson, with his oversized cranium, diminutive frame, dwarf-like body, had the overall appearance of a youth in his early teens—if not a superannuated child.[45]

Gray could have filled in for many hours with such stories,

humorous or somber, and given a lively touch to many events to which he had been witness, but he was not inclined to open up on the personalities of the nineties, on a closed period of his life. Even the books from the nineties that stood on the shelves of his library were placed so their titles faced in toward the wall. It was no secret, though, that every year he celebrated a special memorial mass for Verlaine on the anniversary of the French poet's death.

During this final period of his life, Gray contributed to *Blackfriars*. Between 1924 and 1934, that Dominican monthly published over a dozen of Gray's original essays. In 1931, he published a small paper-covered book entitled *Poems*. As though to prove that he had completely rung down the curtain on the past, Gray abandoned the stylistic techniques he had used to advantage some thirty-eight years before in *Silverpoints*. *Poems* is marked by prosodic techniques resembling, to some extent at least, those of Gerald Manley Hopkins. Like Hopkins, Gray experimented with both diction and meter. And like Hopkins, Gray wrote of nature activated by the Holy Spirit.

Gray's interest in nature in all its varied moods was stimulated by the many walking tours that he took now and again. He especially loved hiking the rolling hills of Banffshire and Aberdeenshire in Scotland and the Cotswolds of England. During one walking trip through the Cotswolds that he took in 1931, he conceived the novella *Park: A Fantastic Story*.

Gray's last published work appeared in 1934. Significantly, it is an obituary article for his lifelong companion, Raffalovich, and was published in the June issue of *Blackfriars*.[46] Raffalovich had died in his sleep on the morning of February 14. Though in his seventieth year, Raffalovich had been in apparent good health and high spirits the evening before when he had attended a lecture given by Eric Gill, who was staying with Gray at the time.

A few days later, Gray said the funeral mass for his departed friend and, as officiating priest, accompanied an entourage from St. Peter's to the cemetery. It was a bitterly cold morning. The mourners were well protected against the weather, dressed as they were in their heavy winter clothing, but Gray wore nothing over his priestly vestments. An icy wind gave Gray a severe chill. A cold developed into pleurisy.

And then shortly after his tribute to Raffalovich appeared in *Blackfriars*, Gray had to be taken to St. Raphael's nursing home. Conscious toward the end, he joined with the priests at his bedside in their prayers for the dying. His last words were an act of contrition. His last act was to nod his head at the name of Jesus.

Canon John Henry Gray died on June 14, 1934.

Chapter Two

Essayist, Story Writer, and Playwright

Contributions to the *Dial*

Like all aspiring young authors, Gray was anxious to see his name in print. His first opportunity came in 1889. Early in that year, he was invited by Charles Shannon, printer and lithographer, and Charles Ricketts, artist, author, and book designer, to contribute to a periodical they were starting. Gray submitted a critical article and a short story; both were accepted.

The first issue of the *Dial*, as Shannon and Ricketts named their journal, appeared in August of 1889. It was composed almost entirely of their work, some work of a fellow artist, Reginald Savage, and the two contributions of Gray. His first piece, "Les Goncourts," was a critical essay on the merits of the Goncourt brothers, his second, an allegorical bit of fiction entitled "The Great Worm."

Over the next few years, Gray remained on the best of terms with Shannon and Ricketts and continued contributing to their periodical. The second number of the *Dial* (1892) contained three of Gray's poems, "Parsifal," "Heart's Demesne," and "Les Demoiselles de Sauve," which he republished a year later in *Silverpoints*. The third number (1893) carried one of his poems, "A Hymn Translated from the Italian of St. Francis of Assisi," and an essay, "Garth Wilkinson." The fourth number (1896) had two of his poems, "The Flying Fish" and "Battledore"; a short story,

"The Beauties of Nature"; and an essay, "The Redemption of Durtal." The fifth and final number of the *Dial* (1897) contained three of Gray's poems, "Leda," "The Swan," and "St. Ives, Cornwall."

Everything that Gray contributed to the *Dial* holds some interest, but of special concern is his first critical essay, "Les Goncourts," and his first short story, "The Great Worm." In addition, his essays on Garth Wilkinson and Joris-Karl Huysmans's fictional counterpart, the Parisian aesthete Durtal, are important to an understanding of Gray's development as a writer. Wilkinson and Huysmans spurred Gray's growing interest in spiritual matters. In Wilkinson's Swedenborgianism, Gray learned about visionary knowledge and a way of producing automatic writing. In Huysmans's Catholicism, Gray discovered the beauties of liturgical art and an absorbing subject for him to reflect upon, religious conversion.

"Les Goncourts"

In his first piece for the *Dial* (1889), "Les Goncourts," Gray did not confine his remarks to the novels of Edmond and Jules de Goncourt; instead, he ranged freely over their entire vision of art and life. To begin with, he considered their concept of the true artist: "always an abnormal creature, a being with an overdeveloped brain, or diseased nerves."[1] Since a good writer is more than "a literary grocer," he must of necessity give vent to his own personality in all that he does. An artist's greatness, the Goncourts held, springs from his very being, from his unique personality "that discovers new motives, and...an earnestness with which to carry them out."[2]

Once this concept of the artist is fully understood, Gray agreed, the sensitive reader has a better chance of dealing with the exacerbated consciousness responsible for the eccentric style of the Goncourts; for "never was great work more destitute of charm for the vulgar than that of MM. Edmond and Jules de Goncourt."[3] If the novels of the Goncourts were beyond certain readers, and even if those readers form a majority, the defect should be sought in the limitations of the readers, not in the novelists' works of art. The Goncourts, it had to be understood, were far too advanced for the multitude. In short, Gray admired the style of the Goncourts for its implied protests against vulgarity. Their willingness to experiment, to violate all conventionality, Gray believed, would be beneficial for English art and literature.

During the last years of the Victorian period, most creative writers were searching for freedom from the trammels of tradition. A regeneration, Gray proposed, required an end to all hostility to the modernity of French art and letters; it demanded as well a new respect on the part of the British public for the artist and his aspirations. "It is quite the rule," Gray maintained, "that the really great only gain their place after fierce struggling; for apart from the actual work, they have to create a taste for it, a task generally tedious in proportion to its worth."[4]

What Gray especially admired about the Goncourts was their neurotic sensibility, their idiosyncratic prose, the haunting melody that sounded throughout all they wrote. Their style was such that Gray, consciously or unconsciously, imitated it throughout his own essay. Impressed with the meticulousness of everything the Goncourts had written, Gray paid lavish attention to his choice of words. He favored strong and strained expressions. At times he even convoluted his syntax, just as the Goncourts had done.

When Gray expatiated on the Philistinism of the British public, for example, he wrote: "And what shall we, we English, say? we the chosen? we who understand so well that a book, to be good, must recount a series of good actions? we who like the shadow thrown across the hero's path only for the pleasure of seeing it swept away again? who feel impatient if the wedding is delayed? Germinie Lacerteux was not married to Coriolis? Put it away! Dear me! if Freddie should get hold of it! Shocking blemishes, happily so soon discovered. Let us beware of the glittering poison."[5]

Gray's writing in the style of the Goncourts added a special touch to his essay, but for him to cover as much as he tried to is a different matter. Inexperienced as a critic, he scattered his best points and failed to develop a central theme. On the positive side, he did distinguish clearly the art of the Goncourts from the realism of Balzac and the naturalism of Zola; moreover, he weighed the contributions of the Goncourts to the novel. He wrote extravagantly of the literary achievements of the Goncourts and also praised them as "literary men influencing the manner of seeing, not thinking, of contemporary painters."[6] It was the Goncourts, Gray emphasized, who made much of the youthfulness in the art of the century, who wrote appreciatively of the Japanese prints that were beginning to influence the best of modern art.

Despite certain shortcomings, "Les Goncourts" is an important bit of criticism.[7] Foremost, in focusing on the work of the Goncourts as he did, Gray properly stressed the value of what was being done by French writers; and he did so ten full years before Arthur Symons published his *Symbolist Movement in Literature* (1899), the first book published in England to introduce such French authors as Huysmans, Mallarmé, Verlaine, and Rimbaud to English readers. Then, too, as an enthusiastic disciple of the Goncourts, Gray, in attacking those who adhered to insular standards, helped foment the aesthetic protest that would so concern artists and writers during the nineties.

As a young, eager poet, Gray was receptive to what was being accomplished by writers on the other side of the channel. His interest was more than simple Francophilia, for the more he read the Goncourts, Baudelaire, Mallarmé, Verlaine, and Huysmans the more convinced he became that France was more aesthetically advanced than England. His enthusiasm would lead him to begin his own personal attempt to domesticate French art—an attempt that would lead him four years later to publish his *Silverpoints.*

"The Great Worm"

In a limited sense, "The Great Worm," which also appeared in the first issue of the *Dial,* complements "Les Goncourts," for it too is concerned with the artist and his aspirations. The title character of this fanciful tale is a harmless dragon which lives "somewhere in the belly of one of those mountain ranges in Central

Asia, with a name as ragged as its silhouette."[8] Unlike the typical dragon, this Great Worm is a mild creature: he "does not snort fire, and none but honeyed words ever leave his gentle lips."[9]

One day the Worm decides to visit a nearby city, where "choosing his steps most carefully, so as not to derange public edifices, and threading himself through triumphal arches with marvelous dexterity,"[10] he arrives at the Royal Palace. After pledging fealty to his Prince, he is commissioned a general. Everywhere the Worm leads his army, peace and order are established.

For reasons unknown even to himself, one fine day he draws his soldiers up in a line. There is a banging of cymbals. Clouds of birds arise, screeching as they cross and circle the sky. From out of nowhere a figure of silent whiteness appears: "She passed over the ripple gold around the city, smoothly as her chariot upon the highways of the city. Her body had the undulations of a pod, ripe swollen to bursting; her breasts were like mounds under moonlit snow. Her hair, gold as corn at noon, was prodigal as a waterfall; and her eyes were like pansies."[11]

Straightaway she approached the Worm to offer him a lily that she bore in her hands. Astonished but highly pleased, the Worm accepts the flower and secures it between the scales of his breast. Without a word, the lovely figure of whiteness turns and departs. The Worm, struck dumb, displays no immediate reaction.

That night, however, he is convulsed by pain. The sentinels are horrified when they see the Worm writhing round and round under the frigid light of the moon, but they can do nothing. They hear him emit a loud, hideous cry: "Why am I a worm?"[12] The following morning his bloody corpse is discovered. Apparently the Worm has died of a broken heart." And the lily upon his breast?— it had taken root there; and the beads of his heart's blood smiled on every petal."[13]

The idea of love bringing about the death of the Worm may not be wholly consistent with the allegory of art that Gray tried to develop. It would almost seem that he meant to confound the reader. For on the one hand, the reader is forced to puzzle over aspects of unrequited love; on the other, he is perplexed by suggestions that what the artist wants to accomplish does not always conform to his own aesthetic vision. Like many another young author, Gray undoubtedly wanted to suggest far more in his tale than he actually could express. If he left his reader somewhat bewildered, so be it. The French Symbolists, whom he so much admired, were never crystal clear in their works. Why, then, could he not be as ambiguous, as cryptic even, in writing about "The Great Worm" as they invariably were in their works?

Realizing the highly enigmatic nature of his tale, Gray appended an epilogue. To hint at meaning he wrote: "A poet lay in a white garden of lilies, shaping images of his fancy, as the river ran through his trailing hair. But in his garden a long worm shook himself after sleep; forgotten his face like a pearl, his beautiful eyes like a snake's, his breathing hair—all. He had complete reminiscences of a worm, and sought the deserts and ravines of dragon loves."[14]

And so, Gray in writing "The Great Worm" ostensibly meant to compose a fable about the aspirations—and frustrations—of the artist, a creature of honeyed words who, wishing only to serve, has but a fleeting moment of glory before being doomed to die of unrequited love.

"Garth Wilkinson"

In "Garth Wilkinson," which appeared in the third issue of the *Dial* (1893), Gray focused clearly on this minor apostle of Swedenborgianism in England. A poet of sorts, Wilkinson not only translated Swedenborg from Swedish into English but composed several works of his own inspired by that mystic. What Gray especially admired about Wilkinson was the quality of imagination he discovered in *Improvisations from the Spirit,* a book of some 109 poems that Wilkinson published in 1857. Without wishing to praise the poet too highly, Gray still compared him favorably with Blake and Wordsworth. "Criticism of Wilkinson will never need to lose itself in eulogy," Gray wrote, "but certain summits in *Improvisations* are signal attainments of imagination."[15]

Whether Gray's meeting with Wilkinson and learning of his ability to produce automatic writing recommended to Gray that he do an article on this strangely gifted poet, or whether Gray met Wilkinson after he wrote his piece cannot be ascertained. But that Gray met Wilkinson sometime late in 1892 or early 1893 can be established.[16] Whenever they met, they must have had a stimulating discussion about writing from influx.

As far as Wilkinson was concerned, there was no great mystery about automatic writing. After a study of Blake, Wilkinson came to conclude that the author of "Songs of Innocence and Experience" wrote the way he did because he was receptive to the Divine Will. Blake, it is true, believed as much, and Wilkinson was prepared to take Blake at his word. If Blake could compose without conscious effort, Wilkinson asserted, then other divinely attuned poets, once they put themselves into a pentacostal frame of mind, could do likewise. The important thing was that initial spark of inspiration to signal the inpouring, the inflow, the influx; then the appropriate words—a gift of tongues—would follow.

In his article on Wilkinson, Gray noted that the author of *Improvisations* claimed in that work that the gift of supernatural dictation required neither "premeditation or preconception, had to be attended by no feeling, and no fervour, but only an anxiety . . . to observe unlooked for evolution."[17] To write by influx, Wilkinson maintained, necessitated prayer to the Creator for "His Guidance, Influx, and Protection."[18]

Wilkinson's gift was a consequence of "Ecstatic Memory," a kind of spiritual infusion in the Swedenborgian sense. "Concerning the speech of angels with man," Gray theorized, "Swedenborg lays down that the thought of man coheres with his memory, and his speech flows from it . . . when an angel or spirit is turned to him and conjoined with him."[19] And then, after examining in some detail Wilkinson's verse, Gray concludes his essay with an analysis of "The Birth of Adam," finding therein spiritual knowledge that came about as a consequence of a pentacostal-like inspiration.

How many poems Gray himself may have attempted through influx is matter for speculation. Some of his shorter devotional

poems, especially a few in his *Blue Calendars*, may very well
have been composed in such a fashion. In any case, through Wilkinson, Gray became curious about the whole question of influx
and creativity; and this curiosity led him to speculate upon the
occult. Interest in the occult led him to Huysmans's *Là-Bas*, one of
the best accounts of occultism and diabolism ever written.

"The Redemption of Durtal"

Huysmans's *Là-Bas* has its hero, Durtal, suspended between the
mechanism of sensation and the void of the spirit. He suffers in a
limbo, unable to reject base materialism. His research into the
life of Gilles de Rais brings him into contact with modern-day
diabolists. Their satanical rites, at which Durtal participates, distract him, but he continually seeks to uncover lost secrets of the
Middle Ages reflective of the unity of the spiritual and the carnal.
At the novel's end, his search is still unresolved, the arcane rubrics
of the Middle Ages apparently having been lost forever. In *En
Route,* a sequel to *Là-Bas,* Huysmans has Durtal resume his
search, but this time the emphasis is on finding some clue to the
meaning of life.

Satanism, Durtal concludes, will end in madness. Art at best
is only a placebo. Where to turn? Can religion give Durtal, intent
upon suicide, a reason for living? Drawn to ecclesiastical art and
the beauty of the liturgy, he comes to accept the church as a hospice
for sick souls. With the help of an understanding priest, he goes
on retreat to a Trappist monastery. At La Trappe, Durtal, under
great stress and with considerable soul-searching, makes his con-
fession, repents, is absolved, and admitted into the fold.

The title of Gray's article, "The Redemption of Durtal," indicates the subject he was most concerned with at the time, repentance. Having his own sinful existence in mind, Gray could
write with understanding of Huysmans's *En Route*. It was Huysmans's "degree of treatment" that allowed Gray to label the novel
"peculiar": "the penitent being a man of profound baseness" with

his "spiritual progress . . . narrated . . . as far as an author dare, and as exhaustively as skill and patience are capable."[20]

In his analysis of Huysmans's fictionalized study of conversion Gray began with the problem of Durtal's spiritual malaise and ended with his acceptance of the Faith. "The record is closely consecutive," Gray commented; "digressions are few and under the direct warranty of M. Huysmans' art."[21] What impressed Gray most about the novel is Durtal's "constantly looking, stupidly, for a miracle to take place in him, a violent destruction of his past, the swift summoning to being of some fruit of long, laborious growth," his craving "in his peculiar vulgarity of his worthlessness, a theatrical sign, an explosion of redemption and miraculous repair, an alchemistic operation in favor of his rag of spiritual disposition."[22]

Gray, obviously, could see his own spiritual problems in those borne by Durtal. He, too, like another Durtal, had been "constantly looking, stupidly, for a miracle to take place in him." Several paragraphs later, Gray, still identifying closely with Durtal, ends his essay with the comment that "at the point of utmost progress in *En Route,* Durtal was still at the beginning of the purgative life, and that even after a very long time he would still be at the beginning."[23]

At the time Gray wrote his article on the French novelist, he had not met Huysmans, but like all young English writers, Gray had been fascinated with Huysmans's *A Rebours,* which he probably read shortly after its publication in 1884. Nor is there any way to substantiate that a later meeting between Gray and Huysmans ever took place.[24] Huysmans may have first learned of Gray shortly after "The Redemption of Durtal" appeared in the *Dial,* for Raffalovich mentioned Gray in a letter to Huysmans dated April 21, 1896.

Raffalovich asked the novelist if he had read Gray's article.[25] Huysmans responded that he had. Though he could not read English, Huysmans had a friend translate the article into French for him. Flattered that Gray had written about him, Huysmans commented that he found Gray's essay of considerable interest;

but he was less than enthusiastic. In Gray's essay, Huysmans found it necessary to add, rather ambiguously, that he discovered signs of "non-comprehension, so frequent among critics, of all the mystical, or simply real, side of the book."[26]

"The Person in Question"

During the years that Gray was contributing to the *Dial* he was also translating and editing quite extensively and submitting creative material to such periodicals as the *Butterfly*, the *Pageant*, and *La Revue Blanche*. Among his more important translations are *A Saint and Others* (1892), four short stories of P. C. J. Bourget that Gray translated from the French, and *Satyros and Prometheus* (1898), a work of Goethe that he translated from the German. Gray's edited works include Michael Drayton's *Nimphidia and the Muses* (1896), *Fifty Songs of Thomas Campion* (1896), and *The Poems and Sonnets of Henry Constable* (1897).

The most important prose work that Gray wrote during this period of his life is a story that he did not publish. Its exact date of composition is not known, but internal evidence suggests that it was written early in the nineties, probably late in 1892. The story is "The Person in Question," one of Gray's most successful pieces of fiction. It was published in 1958, shortly after being found among Gray's papers and manuscripts in the Dominican Chaplaincy, Edinburgh, where they had been consigned after his death twenty-four years before.[27]

Why had a typed manuscript certified by Gray to be "a true copy" never before been published? That Gray preserved the work among his private papers for more than forty years rules out any supposition that he may have withheld the story for literary reasons. Why had he hidden it away? Did he hope for its posthumous publication? It would seem that Gray did not publish the story during his lifetime because it would serve to link him to Wilde. Indeed, "The Person in Question" has much in common with *The Picture of Dorian Gray*.

In Wilde's novel, the hero's portrait becomes a faithful record of his sins and iniquities, while his person remains young and un-sullied. In Gray's story, the narrator perceives a pitiful portrait of himself, of his empty vain life, in a future period in which all he has to look forward to is old age and regret. The perception of Gray's narrator is Gray's own vision of himself in his declining years, aimlessly doing the same things of which he had already grown tired. Such a revelation, Gray's insight into himself, accounts for his choosing the path to Rome.

At the time that Gray wrote "The Person in Question," it is apparent, he had an obvious dread of continuing in his dissolute ways, of drifting into an even more meaningless old age, of living his whole life without purpose or direction. It follows that his story is more than just another amiable bit of fiction. The work is highly autobiographical, virtually confessional, and is, in essence, an imaginative handling of the doppelgänger theme with a certain flavor of *Dorian Gray* about it. Little wonder that "The Person in Question" entices and baffles, reveals and conceals, suggests and recommends all sorts of meanings.

The story begins at the Café Royal. Here, one day in late August or early September, the narrator confronts the person in question. He cannot recall the exact day, but he remembers that it was miserably hot. During lunch he overhears a soft voice com-ing from someone sitting at a neighboring table. Anyone else might have thought the voice that of an individual slightly intoxicated or half asleep; the narrator recognizes its pitch as similar to the timbre of his own voice.

Curious, the young boulevardier turns to look at the individual from whom the disturbing voice has come. "I knew the person knew I looked at him, though he seemed not to notice; but I stared steadily. I am not particular on this point; I know when I am at liberty to stare, not to mention the fact that people stare at me enough, people, too, who know better."[28]

The narrator observes a figure about his own proportions, even like him in face, except that this mysterious individual is at least twenty-five years older and has a straggly beard. An exact likeness between them is obscured by the added years and beard. Perplexed, the narrator pauses to consider what he at first supposes to be merely an apparition. Coincidences can only reach a certain point within safe and normal limits, he reasons, and he remains baffled by the distinct gestures and turns of phrase of the older man.

Except for age and a certain repulsiveness, the person in question is twin to the narrator. "Yet, though his voice, manner, and sequence of acts were my own, his movements did not follow mine seriatim. I took trouble and arranged tests to be sure of this."[29] The person begins to follow the narrator through the streets, to cafés, to the theater and social gatherings. Week after week, whenever he dines in public he comes across the person in question.

After at first being amused by his doppelgänger, the narrator grows anxious. The person is not an apparition, and the character fears that "in some near or remote sense *he is myself*."[30] Finally, the narrator comes to feel a solicitude for and dependence upon his other self.

One day, several months later, the person in question does not make his usual appearances. His absence disturbs the narrator, who sulks about, more anxious and confused than before. To distract himself, he goes to an exhibition. In his wandering about the fairground, he unexpectedly meets the person at a roller coaster. He is aghast that the person is seated on the coaster beside a strange woman. A sudden waft of her cheap perfume across the still, dusty air makes the narrator turn his head with revulsion and hate. Realization that the woman drenched in *foin coupé* is a common streetwalker causes him to recoil in shock. Horrified almost to the point of hysteria, he flees the exhibition. A few days later, however, he begins roving the streets in a desperate search for the mysterious stranger.

"I have never seen him since. Days and evenings and nights I passed, haggard, looking for him. My senses grew painfully keen as I strained sight and hearing for a trace of him. I could not bear to be in a place where there was a door, and a possibility of his entering behind me. I would even snuffle at times, in my despair, for a waft of the dreadful scent, that *foin coupé*."[31] At night the narrator is unable to sleep. In complete agony he keeps berating himself: "What shall I do? What shall I do?"[32]

"What shall I do, indeed? That is the tragedy of my life now: what shall I do? I am so broken in health that I have every cause for concern."[33] Whatever the cost, the narrator vows, "I must find him, or know why I ever saw him, who he was, and something about him."[34] But the story concludes with the full fury of such unanswered questions still tormenting the narrator.

In the same way that his narrator is tormented by the enigma of the person in question, Gray was tormented by the fragmentation of his own personality. Just as the narrator grapples with his doppelgänger, Gray tried to grapple with the duality of his own life. The more he played the part of a Dorian Gray, the less the role meant to him. What should he do?

Toward the end of 1892, Gray began to realize that a break with Wilde was imminent. In the same year, Gray had been introduced to André Raffalovich by Arthur Symons. The close friendship that sprung up between Gray and Raffalovich was of no particular concern to Wilde. He had already taken up with Lord Alfred Douglas and was beginning to experience success as a playwright.

How Gray regarded Douglas, how Douglas in turn looked upon Gray, how Raffalovich looked upon Wilde and Wilde in turn regarded Raffalovich, and how all four principals may have interacted with each other is too complex a problem to pursue here. How others looked upon the four figures is likewise too involved an issue for present analysis. What is germane, however, is a comment Arthur Symons made in one of his essays about the habitués of the Café Royal—the very place where Gray's narrator first meets his doppelgänger—and the air of unreality that surrounded Wilde and Gray.

"Nor must I omit to mention Oscar Wilde, an apparition; sometimes with John Gray, another apparition," Symons wrote.[35] The fact that Wilde and Gray struck Symons as apparitions is noteworthy inasmuch as both wrote about apparitions of sorts themselves, Wilde in his *Dorian Gray* and John Gray in "The Person in Question." *The Picture of Dorian Gray* was of course well known to Symons, but there is little chance that he knew of "The Person in Question."

Whatever part Gray plays in Wilde's *Dorian Gray*, the figure of Wilde, to some extent at least, can be discerned in "The Person in Question." When Gray wrote his story, Wilde, nearing forty, had grown fat and foolish. More than likely, Wilde had begun to appear morally repulsive to Gray. The narrator's disgust with the person in question when he discovers him with the harlot at the exhibition is Gray's perception of himself becoming another Wilde—not the witty Wilde who was able to charm everyone he met, but the Wilde who had taken up with roughs, renters, and stable boys. If Wilde enjoyed "feasting with panthers," that was his concern; but Gray wanted no part of such a life-style. Dealing with the turpitude of his own life was difficult enough for Gray.

The person in question, it becomes increasingly obvious, is Gray's future self, the pathetic image of a dandy grown old. In *Dorian Gray*, the dandy remains young and handsome while his portrait grows old and ugly. In "The Person in Question," the narrator is allowed to see himself as he will be in twenty-five years, an effete, blighted, depraved individual. Gray could relish playing the role of a young and adventurous Dorian, but he could not deal with the prospect of his growing older into a morally bankrupt Oscar Wilde.

Though "The Person in Question" was not a major effort on Gray's part, he must have had some regard for the piece to have preserved it for so many years among his private papers and manuscripts. Having put so much of himself into the story, he could hardly dismiss it as just another literary exercise. Unfortunately, neither he nor any of his close friends who may have read "The Person in Question" expressed any critical judgments on the work. Had any such judgments been rendered, the uniqueness of Gray's handling of the doppelgänger would undoubtedly have been singled out as the one factor that sets the story apart. Other nineteenth-century writers had used the theme quite often, few to the same degree or as effectively as had Gray.

Readers who know of Gray, Wilde, and the autobiographical nature of "The Person in Question" can appreciate the story more fully than a reader who may simply happen upon it. The echoing question that brings the story to its close—"What shall I do? What shall I do?"—is especially meaningful to anyone knowledgeable of Gray's contemplation of suicide at the time he was writing the story. But even a reader unacquainted with the confessional aspects of the story can still appreciate its fine use of language, its tension, suspense, and highly emotional ending. Finally, to label "The Person in Question" a most compelling work of fiction, one that makes excellent use of the doppelgänger theme, is hardly an exaggeration.

Playwright Manqué

In addition to writing poetry, fiction, and essays for the *Dial* and translating for various publishers, Gray, early in the nineties, was also writing plays. In 1894, he completed his first drama, a one-act play he entitled *Sour Grapes*. Raffalovich had also written a one-act play entitled *Black Sheep*. To stage both works, Raffalovich rented the West Theatre, Albert Hall, for a dual performance. On April 17, 1894, *Sour Grapes* and *Black Sheep* were performed before a select audience.[36]

The program noted that both plays were musical productions. *Sour Grapes* is further described as "A Masque, Written Entirely in Rhymed Couplets...with Music by F. Gilbert and C. Dick"; *Black Sheep*, as "A Pantomime Pastoral, With Spoken Prologue and Epilogue...Concluding with a Dance...with Music by C. Dick."[37]

How these playlets may have been received by the handpicked audience before whom they were performed cannot be determined. Nothing about the occasion was recorded. Neither play was ever published, nor, apparently, were the manuscripts or prompters' copies preserved. Gray and Raffalovich, so it would seem, must have received some encouragement from their friends; for shortly after their initial contributions to the theater, they made plans to present a full-length drama they were jointly writing. In their youthful enthusiasm, they looked forward to their work being the hit of the season.

Who contributed what, or how the play was finally put together, is not known. More than likely, it was a collaborative effort from beginning to end. Neither ever claimed a greater share of the writing.

Though they dreamed in fire, they worked in clay, and they both later came to repudiate their efforts. One reason was its disagreeable subject—blackmail. Another, undoubtedly, was the mauling it received from critics.

When the curtain goes up on *The Blackmailers*, as Gray and Raffalovich entitled their play, the main character, Claude Price, is full of virtuous sentiment. Struggling against temptations, he exerts a modicum of effort to control his proclivity toward evil; but not for long. He obtains a sinister influence over a foolish youth, Hal Danger. Both Claude and Hal are members of influential families. Prodigal sons, they cannot live within their allowances. Out at the elbows as they are, without cash or credit, they stoop to blackmail.

They levy blackmail right and left, but without much success. When Claude is threatened with criminal prosecution, he thinks first of taking poison; but upon reflection he decides to fall back on his family for help. In the last act, after he is firmly berated by them, they recommend that he emigrate. Their proposal he rejects as one worse than poison. He walks out on a family council after seriously offending an uncle and an aunt, a cousin, and even his own mother. Shortly before the final curtain descends, his mother, confused and deeply wounded by her son's behavior, questions how such a blackguard could be her child, how he could so disgrace his family.

The plot so summarized may suggest a comedy that Wilde could have used for one of his plays—but wisely rejected. Gray and Raffalovich, however, were not interested in comedic effects; indeed, in their writing of *The Blackmailers*, they wished to exploit the abnormal and the bizarre. They wanted their drama to be in the vein of Ibsen, and they made sure that the final curtain would descend on that note of interrogation so favored by Ibsenites. *The Blackmailers*, so they believed, was a substantial drama worthy of serious critical attention.

With dreams of applause ringing in their ears, they looked forward to the presentation of *The Blackmailers* at the Prince of Wales Theatre. The curtain went up on a matinee performance on June 17, 1894. When the curtain later fell, they undoubtedly heard polite applause from their friends, but they received little acclaim from the critics.

A critic for the *Times*, for example, could find little to praise about the "new and original play...tried at the Prince of Wales Theatre." After summing up the plot, he wrote of the acting being in the hands of an excellent company. For some reason, he did not commit himself other than to note that *The Blackmailers* was "without precedent and may very well hope to remain without imitators"; but even through understatement he made it clear that he found the play a major disappointment.[38] Other critics were less indulgent.

Gray and Raffalovich would have been wise to forget *The Blackmailers* and move on to something else, but in an effort to blunt harsh criticism, they wrote to the drama critic of the *Illustrated London News* and projected blame for failure, not on the play itself, but on its faulty production. "I may be very stupid," the critic responded, not privately to Gray and Raffalovich but in an open letter to the readers of the *Illustrated London News*, "but I do not quite understand the assumptions of the young authors of *The Blackmailers*, two able and enthusistic young men, fond of the stage, students of dramatic literature in all countries, but who, having written a play on a disagreeable subject, turn round and say, 'It is no child of mine.'"[39]

Nor was the critic for the *Illustrated London News* alone in his bewilderment. A critic for the *Theatre* also entered the fray after

Gray and Raffalovich wrote to him. First he stated their side: "It was, they assert, only 'a mangled and mutilated version'... ruined by cuts, omissions, impoverishments and slipshod.' "[40] But then he rebutted their position. Imagine a book by Tennyson or Meredith, he continued, being disclaimed and blaming the printers. If they ever did such a thing, the public would still hold them responsible. So, too, must the authors of *The Blackmailers* take full responsibility for their play: "Would they not have claimed it as their own if, despite any 'managerial' chances, it had been successful?"[41]

When at last it became painfully obvious that the more they tried to defend *The Blackmailers*, the more critics were going to hold its authors fully responsible, Gray and Raffalovich let the matter drop.

Two Short Duologues

Instead of writing another weighty Ibsen-like drama, Gray and Raffalovich decided to experiment with two short duologues, *A Northern Aspect* and *The Ambush of Young Days*. Both plays were published together in May 1895 in a forty-page booklet that its authors meant only for their friends.[42]

The title page contains the words "Privately printed and not for general distribution," a code term that translates into "Not for critical review." Having suffered sufficiently at the hands of the critics, Gray and Raffalovich did not want their duologues to be reviewed. They knew, furthermore, that their latest dramatic efforts could hardly command the London stage, that it was foolhardy to allow their work to be contrasted with the plays of Wilde, Ibsen, or other successful playwrights.

A Northern Aspect and *The Ambush of Young Days* were performed privately at one or another of Raffalovich's social gatherings. Both plays have some merit and were probably enjoyed by their select viewers. Who among the friends of Gray and Raffalovich would not have been pleased with an hour or so's dramatic diversion in a comfortable Mayfair drawing room?

When the curtain goes up on *A Northern Aspect*, Lady Augusta

Smalz, an attractive widow, has just become engaged to Sir Charles
Wren, a highly eligible bachelor. When the curtain falls, they
have mercifully discovered how completely incompatible they are.
Little really happens. The brevity of the play, in fact, does not
allow for much plot twisting, character development, or dramatic
conflict. What its authors could do within the limits of the play
was to entertain with clever dialogue; and that is about all they did.

At one point, for example, after apparently agreeing on everything from colors to religion, Sir Charles and Lady Augusta even
cover their mutual dislikes: scenery, cigars, cycling, and all displays of affection. But they cannot quite come to terms about
Hoffman, Sir Charles's cat. "He will be one more link between
us," Sir Charles recommends. "I suppose you are not one of those
women who squirm if a cat speaks to them."[43]

Lady A: What makes you say that?
Sir   C: Well, the truth is, they are so restless, and Hoffman gets
         nervous when people fidget about. Seeing them move would
         keep him awake, and he requires a deal of sleep at his age.
Lady A: I may get rid of the birds, possibly; as I have a very nice
         parrot.
Sir   C: We shouldn't mind a *talking* parrot.
Lady A: I don't hold much to the birds. They're not company for my
         dear poodle.
Sir   C: I like going for a walk with a poodle, but Hoffman can't
         bear dogs that know tricks. Now isn't a poodle dangerous
         at times...
Lady A: No. never.[44]

Their discussion about animals exhausted, Sir Charles introduces
the subject of his enamels and glazes, his china. And after more in-
nocuous dialogue, he suddenly realizes how truly tyrannical Lady
Augusta really is. Just as suddenly, she discovers she cannot tolerate
Sir Charles because he is too much of an artist. To break their
engagement, he suggests that Lady Augusta think about marriage
to Mr. Phillimore. After all, Mr. Phillimore is so much more simple

than Sir Charles. Lady Augusta agrees. With a polite kiss of her hand, Sir Charles exits and the curtain comes down.

The Ambush of Young Days, like *A Northern Aspect*, also concerns a young couple and their engagement. Again there is little plot and less character development. One day, Belle, a "new woman," dares to broach the subject of marriage to Tom, an aspiring poet. Somewhat shocked but not unagreeable, Tom accepts Belle's proposal.

Admiringly, she focuses on his latest volume of puerile poems. "What! are *Gasflowers* really going to be published? and on fog-coloured paper?" she asks. "And have you designed your own frontispiece yet, with the girl climbing up a lamp-post?" To which Tom responds with a great deal of enthusiasm: "I shall have to write something about you.... I know what I'll do. I'll dedicate the lot to you."[45]

After a while, Tom, skillfully led by Belle, concludes, "Marriage is the answer to so many questions."[46] In their final exchange of sentiment, Tom wonders aloud if perhaps they have not invented marriage.

B: Yes, I feel as though we had discovered America or a new element. But are you sure you will never regret?

T: My charming wife, my sweet friend, how could I? Are you not my ideal? And you do care for me? Of course you do? Of course you do. Besides...

B: Besides?

T: Nothing.

B: Tell me.

T: Well, besides, we are young and sensible minded, are we not?

B: Of course we are.

T: Then marriage is for us.

B: It is not a prison or a cage.

T: It is only a ring for you.

B: And an unfading buttonhole for you.

T: An offensive and defensive alliance.

B: A truce.

T: And the whole of life before us.

Curtain[47]

To dismiss such dialogue as banal or pointless is to forget that audiences at the turn of the century relished such meaningless verbal exchange. Meaninglessness in such a mode was considered almost an end in itself. After all, Wilde had succeeded with similar verbal wit, and Gray and Raffalovich were imitating the vacuous dialogue that had made Wilde's plays so appealing to Victorian theatergoers. In their writing of *A Northern Aspect* and *The Ambush of Young Days*, Gray and Raffalovich had tried to please a select, sophisticated audience, and to a certain extent, they succeeded. Any success they may have enjoyed was dimmed, however, by the dramatic achievements of Wilde.

Before Gray wrote *Sour Grapes* and collaborated with Raffalovich on *The Blackmailers, A Northern Aspect*, and *The Ambush of Young Days*, he imagined that writing for the theater would be both fun and profitable. Ever present in his mind was Wilde's meteoric rise as a playwright. Overlooking *The Duchess of Padua* and *Vera*, two of Wilde's dramatic failures, he thought mainly of the tremendous reception accorded *Lady Windermere's Fan* and *A Woman of No Importance*.

Only after Gray tried to emulate Wilde—and failed—did he come to the realization that Wilde possessed a dramatic genius and that he did not. The plays that Gray wrote by himself and in collaboration with Raffalovich, if compared with the dramas of Wilde, can properly be dismissed as "little more than ... experiments of gifted amateurs."[48] To controvert such critical judgment would be difficult, if not unreasonable. And yet, if the theater proved not to be Gray's medium, he could take comfort from the reputation he had achieved as a poet. In 1893, his *Silverpoints* had made him one of the most talked-about poets of the nineties.

Chapter Three

The French Influence and *Silverpoints*

At the Bodley Head

Early in 1892, after translating several works of the French Symbolists and writing poems of his own in their manner, Gray gave some thought to gathering the best of his efforts into an anthology of sorts. The Bodley Head, he knew, was willing to publish young poets of talent and fashion. He decided to try his poems with John Lane and Elkin Mathews, founders of one of the most unusual publishing houses in the history of printing. On May 27, Gray strolled up Vigo Street to the Bodley Head office to discuss his poetry with Lane, but Lane was out. Disappointed but not discouraged, Gray left "a roll of poems."[1] A few days later, he called again, and this time found Lane in his office. After a pleasant chat about art and literature, a discussion of Gray's poetry ensued.

Lane, who had been publishing the works of young, controversial writers since 1887, was not unenthusiastic about Gray's poetry. The Bodley Head had advertised itself as "Publishers and Vendors of Choice and Rare Editions in Belle Lettres," and it seemed that Gray's projected book of poetry would satisfy the primary goal of producing beautiful books of lasting quality. On June 18, after having given careful consideration to Gray's "roll of poems," Lane ar-

46

rived at a favorable decision.[2] Agreements were reached to publish a limited edition of 250 copies and a deluxe edition of 25 more.

Charles Ricketts, it was decided, would design the work. Although only twenty-six years old at the time, Ricketts was one of the few creative book designers in London. A true artist, he believed that a good book should be "a living and corporate whole, the quality of beauty therein ... all pervading."[3] Unlike most Victorian book jobbers, Ricketts maintained that every well-written volume had to be made as beautiful as possible, "like any other genuine work of art."[4] Accordingly, he recommended that Gray's delicate poems be printed in minute italics on handmade Von Gelder paper with extra-wide margins. Then, too, the entire volume would have to be uniquely bound.

When finally published in March 1893, Gray's first book of poetry as designed by Ricketts proved to be one of the most individualistic and representative works of the English Decadence. Inside and out the book is a masterpiece, and the title of that masterpiece is *Silverpoints.*

Physically, this landmark of nineties' verse is one of the most beautiful books Ricketts ever designed.[5] *Silverpoints* is tall and very slender (11 by 22 centimeters), bound in green cloth, and adorned with wavy gold lines running from top to bottom. Superimposed upon the lines of the front and the back covers are sixty-six flame like willow leaves and blossoms, also in gold. The green and gold have special meaning, for in virtually each poem of the twenty-nine making up the volume, there is some allusion to nature or plants; but as though to imply the superiority of art over nature, the gold pattern dominates the green color.

The book's title suggests a superior and subtle art technique, that of silverpointing. A gifted artist himself, Gray knew that the silverpoint had been used by such masters as Botticelli and Dürer to create delicate drawings. Possibly he had experimented with silverpointing himself; the required stylus and especially prepared oxide paper were readily available. Certainly he was familiar with the art of his contemporaries Alphonse Legros and Edward Burne-Jones and the remarkable silverpoint effects they had achieved in some of their best drawings. But the significance of *Silverpoints* lies beyond its clever title, its unique binding, its fastidious italic type.

Not for Popular Consumption

Gray intended *Silverpoints* to be circulated mainly among his friends and members of the avant-garde. The very nature of his art precluded popular consumption, and he must have been surprised at all the attention his work ultimately received. As originally planned, Wilde was to be presented with the first copy, for the author of *Dorian Gray* had intended to subvene publication costs. For whatever reason, however, an agreement that Wilde had made with Mathews and Lane was abrogated.[6] Wilde was not the kind of individual to go back on his word, and conjecture allows the inference that it was Gray who nullified the original contract.

Silverpoints was to have been published in the autumn of 1892; it was not published until the spring of 1893. Gray simply required time to revise his manuscript. Among the more important revisions that he finally made was the deletion of two poems, "Song of the Stars" and "Sound."

Lane was the one who had first recommended to Gray that "Song of the Stars" be deleted. Though he often dared publish material that other editors would not handle, Lane felt squeamish about this poem. When he notified Gray, who undoubtedly desired to be bold and wicked, to shock and attract attention, the poet acquiesced. "By all means," he replied, "omit 'Song of the Stars' from *Silverpoints*."[7] Later, Lane also had misgivings about "Sound." Gray did not believe either poem was especially indelicate, but as a neophyte poet he had no choice but to comply with Lane's strictures.

When "Song of the Stars" was finally published in 1932 it created little stir.[8] "Sound," however, has had an entirely different history. It first appeared in print in 1926, and A. J. A. Symons, who was responsible for its publication, attributed it to Gray. Gray did not deny that he was its author, nor did anyone else come forth to challenge its attribution. After his death, Gray's sister (whose religious name was Sister Mary Raphael), upon being questioned by an American scholar,[9] maintained that she was familiar with virtually everything that her brother had written but that she had no knowledge of "Sound." She preferred to believe that Gray had not written the poem, but he had.[10]

One fact among all sorts of speculations remains: the original contract covering the publication of *Silverpoints* was invalidated. A new agreement was drawn up on January 4, 1893, and Mathews and Lane decided to publish *Silverpoints* at their own expense. In venturing to issue Gray's poems in a limited edition without Wilde's subvention, Mathews and Lane did not assume much of a risk. They reasoned the volume would attract considerable attention, that they would be able to dispose of all copies.

Silverpoints could hardly be ignored. A critic for the *Graphic* wrote of Gray as a talented young poet who "shows in his *Silverpoints* . . . that if he would abandon the affectation of contemporary French verse, he might write excellent English poetry."[11] A critic for the *Pall Mall Gazette* echoed the same thought, but going a step further, he castigated Gray as *"Le Plus Decadent des Decadents."*[12] Richard Le Gallienne, who also questioned the Francophilia of the English Decadents, did not know what to make of the work. Unable to praise *Silverpoints* and unwilling to carp, he fired a Parthian shot: "Really, Mr. Gray must check these natural impulses."[13]

Ada Leverson, at loggerheads with Le Gallienne, thought it well that Gray had followed his "natural impulses." Drawn to the elegance of the volume, she especially admired the wide expanse of white on each page framing each poem. She quipped: "There was more margin; margin in every sense . . . and I remember . . . when I saw the tiniest rivulet of text meandering through the very largest of the meadow of margin, I suggested to Oscar Wilde that he should go a step further . . . ; that he should publish a book all margin; full of beautiful unwritten thoughts. . . ."[14]

Gray's other friends and acquaintances also had their say, but none could match the cleverness of Ada Leverson. Robert Hichens made a special effort to do so, however. In *The Green Carnation,*

his brilliant satire of the period and of Wilde, Lord Alfred Douglas, and others in their circle who had actually appeared in public
wearing carnations dyed green, Hichens put all sorts of quasi-
aesthetic gibberish into the mouths of Esmé Amarinthe (Wilde)
and Lord Reggie Hastings (Douglas); but he left it to Mrs.
Windsor, the ideal society hostess, to comment on Gray's poetry.
In her carefully considered opinion, "*Silverpoints* was far finer
literature than Wordsworth's *Ode to Immortality* or Rossetti's
Blessed Damozel."[15] Her proclivity was for preciosity and obscurity in verse, for Mrs. Windsor loved "sugar and water, especially
when the sugar was very sweet and the water very cloudy."[16]

Hichens obviously meant to disparage the new aesthetic, to
laugh it out of existence, but his comments on *Silverpoints* in *The
Green Carnation* served only to help Gray's first volume of poetry
become one of the most precious diadems of fin-de-siècle literature.

Selective and Memorable

To keep his first book of poetry selective and memorable, Gray
limited the volume to twenty-nine poems. Sixteen of the total
number were original; thirteen, translations. Among the translations are seven "Imitations" from Verlaine, three from Baudelaire,
two from Rimbaud, and one from Mallarmé. And as had Verlaine
before him, Gray dedicated particular poems to friends and acquaintances, to a prominent actress, and even to a genuine princess.
Oscar Wilde, Ernest Dowson, Frank Harris, Jules La Forgue,
Pierre Louÿs, and Verlaine were among the men of letters so
honored. The actress was Ellen Terry, whom Gray greatly admired,
the member of royalty, Princesse de Monaco.

For an epigraph, Gray chose the words "... *en composant des
acrostiches indolents*." Those familiar with French poetry recognized the letters *P.V.* appended to the epigraph as the initials of
Paul Verlaine. Readers of Verlaine may even have recalled the
poem from which the words were taken—"*Langueur*." Gray's choice
of such an unusual inscription is a clear indication that he approved
of the decadent languor of Verlaine's poetry, and that he too, like

Verlaine, would create, poetically, an atmosphere of dreamlike sloth. Gray's "indolent acrostics" would be crafted, furthermore, with all the care and ingenuity that Verlaine exercised in the writing of his verse.

That general sense of languor that Gray aimed for pervades most of the poems in *Silverpoints*, but in subject matter and style they run a wide gamut. To categorize them is difficult. Some celebrate evil; a few are devotional. Indolent languor is offset by intense passion in those poems that treat of venereal themes. As though to steep the emotions in all that is sensuous and sensual, Gray mingled images of honey and roses, purple breasts and golden hair, founts of pleasure and tears of pain throughout the lines of those poems that explore unchecked nature and depraved beauty. In the more delicate and less decadent works, there is a denial of the grossness of matter and a glorification of the spirit.

Several of the poems, moreover, can be read as self-conscious critiques of inherited aesthetic assumptions about autonomous art and impoverished nature. Then, there are two or three poems that are definite prototypes of Imagism. Others proclaim the beauty and peace of an ideal world even while lamenting that such are beyond human attainment. The few sonnets are mannered imitations of Elizabethan love verse. In short, the poems in *Silverpoints* fly off in all different directions, but their unique point of convergence is a dandiacal aloofness: in their dreamlike mood they avoid clear statement, commitments of any kind or degree.

In common with other poets of the fin de siècle, Gray had a gift of epithet, of rhythm, of symbol, of color. But his perspectives were highly individual. His original poems are marked by singularity and subtlety. In his so-called "Imitations," Gray had the ability to reproduce with surprising exactitude the rhythms and most complex measures of his models. Most of his English renditions of difficult French poems are more than masterpieces of technique, however; for, more often than not, he could capture the spirit of the original and transmute it into striking English verse. At times, his translations convey the chief characteristics of the original; other times, Gray's individuality breaks through. And that is why he preferred to place the term "Imitated from the French" at the head of his renditions from the works of Verlaine, Baudelaire, Rimbaud, and Mallarmé—the poets he most admired.

Nature Beholden to Art

The lead poem in *Silverpoints* is "Les Demoiselles de Sauve." Just as the character Des Esseintes in Huysmans's *A Rebours* fabricates flowers and prefers his artificial creations to real blossoms, Gray, too, in this poem exalts the artificial over the real. The Princesse de Monaco, to whom Gray dedicated the work,[17] was pleased that the poem suggests that she possessed the beauty and the mystery of the Demoiselles he writes about, that there is an inexplicable quality in some women superior even to a Provençal garden in spring.

The opening stanza and the final stanza frame a picture of three beautiful ladies in an orchard. The second stanza dwells on "proud Jacqueline"; the third, on "High-crested Berte"; and the fourth, on Ysabeau, who "follows last, with languorous pace." All three excite the imagination. What is there about Jacqueline's hennaed fingertips that can cause pale blossoms to blush? Does the term *high-crested* used to describe Berte refer to her coiffure or the allure of a full, high bosom? Are her slant, clinched eyes, which are probably heavily dashed with mascara, meant to belie her delicate hands clasped in prayer? And why does Ysabeau backward stoop to press, voluptuously, a bunch of eglantine to her full, sensuous lips?

So alluring are these self-conscious ladies of Sauve, they command the attention of nature, as though nature is beholden to art.

> Pale blossoms, looking on proud Jacqueline,
> Blush to the color of her finger tips,
> And rosy knuckles, laced with yellow lace.
>
> High-crested Berte discerns, with slant, clinched eyes,
> Amid the leaves pink faces of the skies;
> She locks her plaintive hands Sainte-Margot-wise.

Ysabeau follows last, with languorous pace;
Presses, voluptuous, to her bursting lips,
With backward stoop, a branch of eglantine.

In the final stanza, this garden, which has been enchanted by Jacqueline, Berte, and Ysabeau, becomes more like a palace as these

Courtly ladies through the orchard pass;
Bend low, as in lord's halls; and springtime grass
Tangles a snare to catch the tapering toe.

The following poem, "Heart's Demesne," also has a garden setting. The heart of a beloved lady, in fact, is depicted as a symbolic garden. As the poet leans over the flowers, each one speaks to him of his rare mistress.

Amaranth fadeless, tells me of thy flesh.
Briar-rose knows thy cheek, the Pink thy pout.
Bunched kisses dangle from the Woodbine mesh.

I love to toll, when Daisy stars peep out,
And hear the music of my garden dell,
Hollyhock's laughter and the Sunflower's shout.

Gray's choice of flowers here is unique and symbolic. And even though the poet hears beautiful music in his garden, the laughter of the Hollyhock and the shout of the Sunflower, mystery still abides. As the final verse reveals, "many whisper things I dare not tell."

"Heart's Demesne" and "Les Demoiselles de Sauve" are similar in structure, both having five three-line stanzas. The rhyme scheme of "Les Demoiselles" is irregular, whereas in "Heart's Demesne," Gray has successfully managed terza-rima. More than likely, he reserved terza-rima for "Heart's Demesne" as a tribute of sorts to Verlaine, to whom he dedicated the poem.

The third work in *Silverpoints* is an innocent, rather insignificant fourteen-line poem entitled "Song of the Seedling." In the first four lines, the poet addresses a seedling, asking: "Why are you joyful? What do you sing?" Have you no fear of "that crawling thing... and the worm?" The seedling, endowed with its own identity, responds in the lines that follow that its chief concern is raindrops that will moisten its roots, that it has "No thoughts of the legged thing, of the worm no fear." Its chief goal is vibrant life.

> Every moment my life has run,
> The livelong day I've not ceased to sing:
> I must reach the sun, the sun.

The following poem, "Lady Evelyn," is a sonnet that could have been written about any real or fancied woman who had "the power to stir" Gray's heart "to every Lust." Among fancied women, Shakespeare's Dark Lady might be a likely candidate. In fact, even though the name *Evelyn* has the etymological meaning of "pleasant," it does suggest "eve," "darkness." And if such theorizing be extended beyond onomastic coincidence, it could well be that this is one of Gray's earliest sonnets written in imitation of Shakespeare. The subject, the meter, the rhyme, the diction, and even the theme support such an inference; but, then, does not every would-be sonneteer begin writing sonnets in the manner of the Bard?

That travail of one sort or another comes into everyone's life is the theme of the next poem, "Complaint." Dedicated to Felix Fénéon, it is structured in four stanzas of four lines each. Gray states that this troublesome quantity that "hast no name" somehow entwines "all things of fragrance and of worth."

> Thou shout! thou burst of light! thou throb
> Of pain! thou sob!
> Thou like a bar
> Of some sonata, heard from far
>
> Through blue-hued veils! When in these wise,
> To my soul's eyes,
> Thy shape appears,
> My aching hands are full of tears.

The theme of "Complaint" recalls the poetry of nuance and regret, of longing and dissatisfaction, that so appealed to Ernest Dowson, Lionel Johnson, and the early Yeats.

The next poem, "A Halting Sonnet," is uniquely Gray himself. Its personal quality is a consequence of Gray's high esteem for Ellen Terry, to whom he dedicated the work. With as much flattery as he could fuse into his fourteen lines, Gray doted upon the "power" of the actress, "a lady, princess, goddess, artist such." As a poet he aspired to sing her praises loud and clear; yet, as he laments in his final couplet,

> The couplet is so great that, where thou art,
> —Thou being a poem—it is past my art.

The following poem, "Wings in the Dark," Gray dedicated to the journalist Robert Harborough Sherard. Gray had met him through Wilde about the same time that he had also met Ada Leverson, Charles Ricketts, Charles Shannon, and other friends of Oscar. Sherard must have made an impression upon Gray for Gray to have dedicated this poem to him. Sherard, who was struggling to make a name for himself as a writer, was pleased, though he was so intent in his devotion to Wilde that he had little time for the author of *Silverpoints*. Theorizing about the reasons Gray dedicated "Wings in the Dark" to Sherard and how Sherard may have responded may have some value; but more important is a consideration of the poem itself.

The "wings" of the title are the sails of a boat that ventures

> Forth into darkness faring wide—
> More silent momently the silent quay—
> Towards where the ranks of boats rock to the tide,
> Muffling their plaintive gurgling jealousy.

Six additional stanzas describe the boat as "she flaps her wings...straining every cord," sailing past "fishers through the darkness," until

Suddenly all is light and life and flight,
Upon the sandy bottom, agate strewn.
The fishers mumble, waiting till the night
Urge on the clouds, and cover up the moon.

"Wings in the Dark" has been read as more than a delightful poem about the sea and sailing. One critic suggests that the meaning involves an artist at loggerheads with nature: "It is too late for the late-Romantic artist to assume a Wordsworthian posture before nature, for nature has become alien and unknowable."[18] If, like the speaker in the narrative, an artist sets out in pursuit of nature, he will return with little more than his own metaphors. Even if the vessel be "transformed into a Pegasus," poetry, if managed at all, will be "by indirection and darkness"—by "Wings in the Dark."[19]

Two Dream Poems

Most of the poems in *Silverpoints* reflect in some degree Gray's dandyism. The next two poems, "The Barber" and "Mishka," have a surrealistic quality. Though quite different in subject matter, both concern reveries and take their origin from Gray's unconscious mind. Within the dream framework of each is an extraordinary boldness of expression. Nightmarish moments are embellished with hallucinatory details appealing to sight, to touch, to taste. The lines quiver with sense imagery that is at times extreme. Gray could not keep his poetic imagination, it would seem, from delving into a psychological cosmos of fatal beauty.

"The Barber" yields multiple meanings. On one level, it is little more than a sexual. fantasy. On another, Gray's artificer, who employs cosmetics, wigs, and exotic dyes to improve upon nature, is symbolical of the Decadent artist whose love of *maquillage*[20] foreruns madness. Ian Fletcher reads the poem as "a parable of the artist; profounder than the mad fetichism of Beardsley's *Carrousel*."[21]

Gray's "Barber" does bring to mind Beardsley's "Ballad of a Barber" and his drawing of *The Coiffing*, both of which Beardsley did for the *Savoy*. The fact that Gray's poem antedated Beardsley's interest in the subject by three years allows the inference that Gray's influence was felt by Beardsley, especially since the young artist was familiar with Gray's *Silverpoints*. Be that as it may, both Gray's "Barber" and Beardsley's "Ballad of a Barber" typify extreme artifice. Possibly Beardsley's poem conveys "a complete allegory of Decadence," as Jerome Buckley has commented,[22] but it is quite inferior to Gray's.

In Gray's poem, in the opening stanza, the speaker dreams that he is a barber whose "trembling fingers" work on "manes extravagant...of many a pleasant girl." It is his task, as he relates in his monologue,

> To gild their hair, carefully, strand by strand;
> To paint their eyebrows with a timid hand;
> To draw a bodkin, from a vase of kohl,
> Through the closed lashes; pencils from a bowl
> Of sepia to paint them underneath;
> To blow upon their eyes with a soft breath.

In the second stanza, the dream grows vague.

> I moulded with my hands
> The mobile breasts, the valley; and the waist
> I touched; and pigments reverently placed
> Upon their thighs in sapient spots and stains,
> Beryls and crysolites and diaphanes,
> And gems whose harsh names are never said.
> I was a masseur; and my fingers bled
> With wonder as I touched their awful limbs.

And then in the third stanza,

> Suddenly, in the marble trough, there seems
> O, last of my pale mistresses, Sweetness!
> A twylipped scarlet pansie. My caress
> Tinges thy steelgray eyes to violet.

Adown thy body skips the pit-a-pat
Of treatment once heard in a hospital
For plagues that fascinate, but half appal.

The poem builds to a crescendo. In the last stanza, the poet's object comes to life. Hearing the sound of the "pit-a-pat" makes his blood stand cold. The "chaste hair" of his mistress ripens into "sullen gold." But that is not all, for

The throat, the shoulders, swelled and were uncouth.
The breasts rose up and offered each a mouth.
And on the belly pallid blushes crept,
That maddened me, until I laughed and wept.

Gray's "Barber," William York Tindall once commented, "exceeds in preciousness all previous celebrations of artifice."[23] He could have added that it is even more "precious" than any other poem that followed.

"Mishka," like "The Barber," has multiple levels of meaning. According to Ian Fletcher, in this poem Gray, mocking his own myth and idiom, presents a comic vision of the Fatal Woman. The Fatal Woman, moreover, "represents the romantic poet's attempt to resolve the antinomies of experience: love-hate, knowledge-mystery, and so on."[24] James Nelson suggests that the parable of "Mishka" is "an objectification of the artist's compelling desire or taste for beauty which leads him away from reality into the sterile world of fatal beauty."[25]

On the narrative level, Mishka is a bear; but a creature that has both brute and human characteristics. In the opening lines, he is dreaming in his wintry cave; outside the world is dark, roots are rotting, and rivers "weep." Though his head be heavy "between his fists," he is still "poet among beasts." During his reverie he perceives monstrous eyes—those of a honeybee—and they turn him into stone.

Wide and large are the monster's eyes,
Nought saying, save one word alone:

> Mishka! Mishka, as turned to stone,
> Hears no word else, nor in anywise
> Can see aught save the monster's eyes.

Honey is under the monster's lips, and Mishka

> follows into her lair,
> Dragged in the net of her yellow hair,
> Knowing all things when honey drips
> On his tongue like rain, the song of the hips.

The monster now becomes "the honey-child," but "the honey-child" is a kind of vampire which rounds Mishka's throat with "the triple coil of her hair." He soon succumbs to the blandishments of paradise as his enchantress strokes "his limbs with a humming sound."

> Of the honey-child, and of each twin mound.
> Mishka! there screamed a far bird-note,
> Deep in the sky, when round his throat
> The triple coil of her hair she wound.
> And stroked his limbs with a humming sound.

At the poem's end, Mishka sleeps on; he remains in a state of sensuous ecstasy. In his dream

> Mishka is white like a hunter's son;
> For he knows no more of the ancient south
> When the honey-child's lips are on his mouth,
> When all her kisses are joined in one,
> And his body is bathed in grass and sun.
>
> The shadows lie mauven beneath the trees,
> And purple stains, where the finches pass,
> Leap in the stalks of the deep, rank grass.
> Flutter of wing, and the buzz of bees,
> Deepen the silence, and sweeten ease.
>
> The honey-child is an olive tree,
> The voice of birds and the voice of flowers,

> Each of them all and all the hours,
> The honey-child is a wingèd bee,
> Her touch is a perfume, a melody.

Communications

"Summer Past" and "The Vines" articulate communications with nature. "Summer Past," which Gray dedicated to Wilde, tells of a season of "Warm hours of leaf-lipped song, / And dripping amber sweat." It was a wonderful time to experience and "sweet to see"; but now other aspects of nature have "their secrecies." Listening well, one might even hear "The beetle humming neath the fallen leaves." In "The Vines," which Gray dedicated to André Chevrillon, he writes of "half-born tendrils" that make their way like a "mottled snake." An intricate rhyme scheme suggests the coiling and interlacing of ivy, bramble, and woodbine in their growth. In four of the five stanzas, the final words in each line rhyme *abbc*; in the middle stanza, the rhyme is *abba*. The rhyme scheme, accordingly, is the same going from the first line to the last or the last to first. Gray's complex interwining of rhyme is an obvious part of his "indolent acrostics."

The next two poems, "Did We Not, Darling?" and "Lean Back, and Press the Pillow Deep," celebrate love. Both, however, have a Poesque quality. In "Did We Not, Darling?" it would appear that the lovers, who once did "walk on earth," are now buried "Deep in the dear dust." Their present state is a thing at last their own, and "none esteem / How our black lips are blackening."

> And none note how our poor eyes fall,
> Nor how our cheeks are sunk and sere...
> Dear, when you waken, will you call?...
> Alas! we are not very near.

The lovers have achieved rest from the troubles in a world where they were scorned and "spat upon," but in death they still are not united. Denied acceptance upon earth, even beyond the grave they are "not very near." All they can think upon is their bodily decay.

The reader is forced to think upon the morbidity of theme. Gray evokes all the senses. There is the song of "fluffy bees" in summer, the visual and olfactory appeal of "spread daffodils" in spring, and the feel of "fresh earth" that surrounds the "frail hearts" of the lovers in a winter of discontent.

In "Lean Back, and Press the Pillow Deep," there are aspects of sensuality combined with suggestions of courtly love. On the sensual plane, the beloved has an enticing smile, a voluptuous line to her cheeks, and a dimple described as "a saucy cave." "Heart's dear demesne," "magic orchard feoff," and "velvet eyne" supply an interesting medieval flavor. A figure out of Poe, the heroine has tired eyes, a pale pallor, and a voice that is tenebrous. Though the lover calls her his with every kiss, he is concerned with "Ephemeral bells." Finally, the reason for pressing the pillow so deeply is made explicit in the last lines:

> Tell me, my dear, how pure, how brave
> Our child will be! what velvet eyne,
> What bonny hair our child will have!

The next poem, "Crocuses in Grass," provides an interesting change of pace. In describing these earliest of spring flowers, Gray used all the color he could work into his sixteen lines.

> Purple and white the crocus flowers,
>   And yellow, spread upon
>   The sober lawn; the hours
> Are not more idle in the sun.
>
> Perhaps one droops a prettier head,
>   And one would say: Sweet Queen,
>   Your lips are white and red,
> And round you lies the grass most green.
>
> And she, perhaps, for whom is fain
>   The other, will not heed;
>   Or, that he may complain,
> Babbles, for dalliaunce, with a weed.

And he dissimulates despair,
>   And anger, and surprise;
>   The white daisies stare
> —And stir not—with their yellow eyes.

Gray's talking flowers are not "fleurs du mal," for what they say is neutral in tone. The personification that begins in the second stanza, however, is a bit strained. Then, too, as Linda Dowling has pointed out, though the rococo delicacy of the crocuses may disguise sensuality somewhat, "the decorously courting flowers... foretoken both Pound's 'gilded phaloi of the crocuses... thrusting at the spring air' and the tumescent vegetation of Lawrence."[26]

The next poem, Gray could have called "Leprous Flowers," but he left it untitled. It reads:

> Geranium, houseleek, laid in oblong beds
> On the trim grass. The daisies' leprous stain
> Is fresh. Each night the daisies burst again,
> Though every day the gardener crops their heads.
>
> A wistful child, in foul unwholesome shreds,
> Recalls some legend of a daisy chain
> That makes a pretty necklace. She would fain
> Make one, and wear it, if she had some threads.
>
> Sun, leprous flowers, foul child. The asphalt burns.
> The garrulous sparrows perch on metal Burns.
> Sing! Sing! they say, and flutter with their wings.
> He does not sing, he only wonders why
> He is sitting there. The sparrows sing. And I
> Yield to the strait allure of simple things.

This well-structured sonnet presents a disturbing vision of external nature. Contrary to Romantic notions, Gray here presents nature as tainted with an almost depraved beauty. His opening quatrain virtually equates nature and evil. Every day an attempt is made to suppress and control unwanted daisies that grow in a formalized garden, but every night they "burst again" and their "leprous stain" remains fresh.

What prompts the young girl in the second quatrain to recall a vague legend about a daisy chain? The reader is left to wonder why the "wistful child, in foul unwholesome shreds" yearns to make "a pretty necklace" of the leprous flowers to wear about her neck. Why, too, should the flowers be "leprous," the little girl "foul"? From Chaucer to Wordsworth, English poets have used the daisy as one of nature's favorite wild flowers. Gray appears to be the only poet to use this common plant in such a Decadent context.

In the sestet, the sun, the leprous flowers, and the foul child form a trinity of unwholesomeness. The sun scorches the asphalt, a symbol of civilization, reminding the reader that the daisies are not growing wild but are intruders into a formal city garden. The leprous flowers, moreover, grow unwanted, unvalued, out of control. As for the child, young as she is, her proclivity is toward evil. Even the birds are symbolic of disordered nature; they are not joyful, chirping in a Garden of Eden, but garrulous visitors that perch on a metal statue of Burns. This statue of the Scottish bard is woefully out of place in this un-Romantic setting.

The intrusive birds, fluttering about, demand that Burns accompany them with his song. He refuses to join their cacaphonous chorus, and sits wondering at his place in so unnatural a garden. Gray the Decadent has set himself against Burns the Romantic: the latter held to the intrinsic goodness of all nature; the former expresses the evil that resides within man and the world about him. The speaker's final thought—"I yield to the strait allure of simple things"—seems a last-minute negation of the depraved beauty of the entire poem.

If the narrative is not provocative enough for the reader, he is free, of course, to infer allegory—something he can do with virtually all the poems making up *Silverpoints*. Is this poem about leprous flowers, for example, concerned with aesthetic limitations, with the poverty of art? Linda Dowling believes that it is. As she reads the work, "the poem subtly relates to the artist's discovery of his role to an abdication of self."[27] Thus the speaker, initially repelled by the crude banality of city garden and city child, finally yields to them. Both the leprous daisies and the foul child, furthermore, are expressive of the sordid and careless assertiveness of natural process.

The little girl, like the decapitating gardener, becomes representative of an artist figure, powerless to control nature's antipathy to the reductiveness of art. In such a reading, the speaker's recognition of his symbolic kinship with the child comes with his vision of another artist, Burns. As everything moves and sings about Burns and the speaker, they remain silent and self-contained, as though fixed by art. When the speaker comes to realize a comic embodiment of his own self-repressed isolation, he abandons his attachment to submerge himself in the mere flux of nature.

An interpretation of this sort juxtaposes the speaker between the flux of nature and the fixity of art. If he yields himself to both experimentally, he need not actually commit himself to either. Discrepancies between literal expression and intended meaning would have to be counterbalanced. Essentially, Gray would seem to be mocking the Promethean fires of Romantic poetry. In mocking what he regards as the threadbare conventions of Romantic verse, moreover, he would be recommending the problematic freedom, anonymity, and severity of the post-Romantic expression. Consequently, as Dowling further recommends, the sources of the poem's "splenetic irony may be found in Baudelaire, in *la névrose* of the Goncourts, and in the *malaise de siècle* of Huysmans."[28] Gray's dandiacal revulsion from the teeming squalor before him would even be suggestive of "the nausea of the twentieth-century existentialist at the pulpy mindlessness of nature, just as the speaker's decision to yield himself to process looks forward to the choices of the existentialist self."[29]

"On a Picture" may also be interpreted as a poem that seeks to merge itself with "the pulpy mindlessness of nature" or "the choices of the existentialist self"; but, basically, it is an Italian sonnet that reads like a poetic rendition of John Everett Millais's

Ophelia. Whether Gray wrote the poem after contemplating Millais's famous painting, or after reading Shakespeare's description of Ophelia's tragic death in Act IV, Scene iv, of *Hamlet*, or after reflecting upon Rimbaud's "Ophélia" cannot be fully determined. Probably all three influenced Gray's poem concerning a picture about a heroine of drama to some degree; but more than likely it was Rimbaud's poem that provided the major spark. Like Millais's painting, Rimbaud's poem treats of the unfortunate Ophelia lying faceup in the water after her suicide.[30]

The subject of Ophelia's death had a special appeal to Gray at the time because of his own Hamlet-like preoccupation with existence and purpose. That the poem is dedicated to Pierre Louÿs is a good indication that even though Gray was in one of the most creative phases of his life, he was still filled with despair. In a letter from Louÿs to Gray dated November 27, 1892, the French poet expressed deep concern over Gray's despondency and his hints at suicide.[31] "On a Picture" allows the inference that Gray, like another Ophelia, desired to free himself from earthly care: "To lie in shadows of shrill river growth, / So steadfast are the river's arms beneath."

Verlaine

The next seven poems are "Imitations" of Verlaine. Gray probably selected these seven poems—and no others—from the many hundreds of verses written by Verlaine for the simple reason that they were the works of the French poet that he most admired. Three of them—"A Crucifix," "Mon Dieu M'A Dit," and "Parsifal"—interestingly enough, are religious; four—"Le Chevalier Malheur," "Spleen," "Clair de Lune," and "Green"—are not. The fact that three of these "Imitations" are of a spiritual nature allows the inference that even though Gray had apparently fallen away from the initial fervor of his conversion to the Church of Rome, he could easily empathize with Verlaine's conversion and find depths of meaning in Verlaine's religious poetry. Though the three devotional poems he decided to include in *Silverpoints* are perhaps as Decadent as they are devotional, they reveal that the spiritual in Gray, as in Verlaine, was at loggerheads with the sensual.

Verlaine had dedicated "Un Crucifix" to Germain Nouveau. Gray dedicated his "Imitation" to Ernest Dowson. Gray's good friend from the Rhymers' Club, like Gray, had also converted to Catholicism and, like the Gray of *Silverpoints*, was at the time less than staunch in the practice of his new faith. If Dowson penned a short note to Gray in gratitude, the letter was not preserved. Privately, Dowson may have pondered the poem's detachment, its lack of personal involvement with its subject. Verlaine's approach was distinct from the spiritual intensity that Dowson manifested in most of his religious poems, in his "Benedictio Domini," for example.

The dandiacal juxtaposed against the religious probably would have found favor with Dowson; but why, he might have questioned, should the words murmured by the Crucified be of such a general nature? Ordinarily one poet would not be captious of any sincere effort that a poet-friend dedicated to him, but Dowson could also have been troubled by the term "Christ's unutterable charm" that Gray used in the fourth line of his translation. "Charm" is an odd bit of poetic diction in a poem descriptive of Christ's hanging upon a cross.

The life-size wooden crucifix "adorned with gold and green" first inspired Verlaine in October 1880. In the opening lines, as rendered by Gray, it stood in "A gothic Church. At one end of an aisle / Against a wall where mystic sunbeams smile / Through painted windows, orange, blue and gold." After an almost rhapsodic description of the crucifix and its surroundings, the poem shifts abruptly to the reality of the event. Verlaine, dilating upon the horror of Golgotha, recalls "The last convulsion of the lingering breath" with which Christ implores "Forgive! Forgive! I perish, let them live." Allusion to "the loving pallor" of Christ's brow, to his "thorny crown," "Broken side," and the nails that have been driven through the hands and feet provide disturbing touches. Effectively yoking the dandiacal and the realistic are the lines:

"The while, to overturn Despair's repose, / And urge to Hope and Love, as Faith demands."

To translate Verlaine faithfully, Gray discovered, was not a simple task. At best, he could only "imitate"; and to "imitate" meant he could take certain liberties, though he took remarkably few with "Un Crucifix." Other than shortening Verlaine's poem from thirty-eight lines to thirty, Gray's translation duplicates its original in meaning and intensity. "A Crucifix" is the kind of spiritual poem that Gray himself could have written, the kind that he would write a few years later in his *Spiritual Poems*.

Gray's translation of Verlaine's "Mon Dieu M'A Dit" complements "A Crucifix." Both poems are sincerely devout in expression; both play out a theme of divine love. In the opening lines of "Mon Dieu M'A Dit," Verlaine has the Crucified say, as rendered by Gray: "Love me, / son, thou must; oh see / My broken side; my heart, / its rays refulgent shine." That love must be learned from suffering, from mystic surrender, is made explicit in the second stanza:

> With thy sins heavy; and my hands;
> > thou seest the rod;
> Thou seest the nails, the sponge,
> > the gall; and all my pain
> Must teach thee love, amidst a world
> > where flesh doth reign,
> My flesh alone, my blood,
> > my voice, the voice of God.

In the concluding stanza, there is a reference to the humanity of Christ and to all men as brothers of the Crucified. Christ's mission as Savior to all humanity is accordingly emphasized in the closing lines:

> Say, have I not loved thee,
> > loved thee to death,
> O brother in my Father
> > in the Spirit son?

Say, as the word is written,
            is my work not done?
Thy deepest woe have I not sobbed
            with struggling breath?
Has not thy sweat of anguished nights
            from all my pores in pain
Of blood dripped, piteous friend,
            who seekest me in vain?

Although "Mon Dieu M'A Dit" may be interpreted in several ways, the primary inference is that Verlaine was intent upon finding spiritual sustenance. In all probability, the poem was inspired by Verlaine's reception of the Eucharist on August 15, 1874, the day he completed the process of his return to full membership in the Christian faith.[32] The "piteous friend" seeking Christ is the French poet himself. Gray, of course, could empathize with the "piteous friend," and regardless of how many verses he might pen on artificial themes and decadent nature—even in a volume having the rather effete title of *Silverpoints*—he, like Verlaine, was anxious for a more meaningful way of life. Both poets might dally with Decadent themes and write highly artificial poetry; but, subconsciously, they had to resolve that age-old conflict between the flesh and the spirit.

The sonnet "Parsifal" reinforces such an interpretation and provides further insight into Gray's interest in Verlaine's religious poetry. Though lacking the spiritual intensity of "Mon Dieu M'A Dit," "Parsifal" is still an exquisite work of art. In his *Confessions of a Young Man*, Moore wrote that he knew of nothing more perfect.[33] A modern critic, in full agreement with Moore, recently described "Parsifal" as being like "a piece of carved ivory or a Renaissance jewel."[34]

Gray knew that "Parsifal" was one of three poems that Verlaine wrote in homage to Wagner; and the admiration that Verlaine had for Wagner, Gray obviously had for Verlaine. In his translation, Gray proved it. The octave of his rendition emphasizes "the flower maidens, and the wide embrace / Of their round proffered arms, that tempt the virgin boy" and focuses on "the Woman Beautiful" and "the fatal charm of her hot breasts." Yet in the sestet are found references to "The holy Javelin that pierced the Heart of God" and the hero's adoration of Christ's "living blood" as found in consecrated "mysterious Wine." In his translation of the sonnet, Gray did not lessen the sensuality or intensify the spiritual in any way. The words in English are essentially those of the original French.

With "Le Chevalier Malheur," however, Gray did take several liberties. Its entire development, in fact, is different from the original. The very first line contains a significant change. Whereas Verlaine opens with "*Bon chevalier masqué*," Gray uses "Grim visor's cavalier!" The lance carried by the knight is not modified by Verlaine; Gray describes it as "unpitying." In the original, the knight speaks to reveal a purpose; Gray omits the words to create an ominous silence, thereby adding a measure of suspense. Verlaine's closing line is "*Au moins, prudence! Car c'est bon pour une fois!*"—the words spoken to him by a policeman on the day of his release from prison. Gray is more direct and meaningful in his conclusion: "Only once can the miracle / avail.—Be wise!" Unfortunately, what Verlaine might have thought about Gray's liberal translation of "Le Chevalier Malheur" into English neither he nor Gray recorded. There is no reason to believe that he would have been less than pleased with any of Gray's emendations.

Nor is it likely that Verlaine was displeased by Gray's translations of "Spleen" and "Clair de Lune."[35] Both give evidence of Gray's ability to imitate Verlaine's lyrical mode. "Spleen" is an extremely good example of Gray's skill in handling Verlaine's octosyllabic verse; but "Clair de Lune," being the better poem, allowed Gray to render the work into remarkable symbolistic verse.

The final "Imitation" from Verlaine is "Green." Conjecture has it that this poem is shot through with recollections of Mathilde, Verlaine's wife. Though separated from her at the time and enmeshed in the life of Rimbaud, Verlaine apparently could not get Mathilde out of his mind. Gray was not unaware of the autobiographical dimensions of "Green," and in his translation he captured the essence of its haunting sensuality:

Leaves and branches, flowers and fruits are here;
And here my heart, which throbs alone for thee.
Ah, do not wound my heart with those two dear
White hands, but take the poor gift tenderly.

I come, all covered with the dews of night
The morning breeze has pearled upon my face.
Let my fatigue, at thy feet, in thy sight,
Dream through the moments of its sweet solace.

With thy late kisses ringing, let my head
Roll in blest indolence on thy young breast;
To lull the tempest thy caresses bred,
And soothe my senses with a little rest.

Mallarmé and Rimbaud

Aware of the extreme difficulties involved in translating Mallarmé, Gray attempted only one "Imitation" of the master Symbolist. Drawn to Mallarmé's "Fleurs" because the poem embodies a measure of Mallarmé's pessimism, his ennui, his fear of sterility, his concern with creativity, Gray was also fascinated by Mallarmé's association of ideas and imagery: past days, flowers, flesh, the moon, the stars as symbols of infancy, virginity, death. He focused on this perfect example of Mallarmé's Parnassian period mainly for the challenges it offered a translator; for the poem incarnates Mallarmé's striving after perfection of form, the mastery of verbal art. And considering how difficult it is to translate Mallarmé, Gray did an admirable job.

Though the "Imitation" may lose something of the richness of imagery and meaning that Mallarmé was able to infuse into his poem, Gray's translation of "Fleurs" is a good example of his own sensitivity to and affinity for Symbolist poetry.

The tawny iris—oh! the slim-necked swan;
And, sign of exiled souls, the bay divine;
Ruddy as seraph's heel its fleckless sheen,
Blushing the brightness of a trampled dawn.

The hyacinth; the myrtle's sweet alarm;
Like to a woman's flesh, the cruel rose,
Blossom'd Herodiade of the garden close,
Fed with ferocious dew of blooddrops warm.

Thou mad'st the lilies' pallor, nigh to swoon,
Which, rolling billows of deep sighs upon,
Through the blue incense of horizons wan,
Creeps dreamily towards the weeping moon.

Praise the censers, praise upon the gong,
Madone! from the garden our woes:
On eves celestial throb the echo long!
Ecstatic visions! radiance of haloes!

Mother creatrice! in thy strong, just womb,
Challices nodding the not distant strife;
Great honey'd blossoms, a balsamic tomb
For weary poets blanched with starless life.

The poem that follows "Fleurs" is Rimbaud's "Charleville." That Gray placed his only translation of Mallarmé between those of Verlaine and those of Rimbaud was not accidental. It was as though he wanted to keep the two poets—who brought such misery into their lives when they were together—apart.

In the opening stanzas, Gray captures the alchemy of Rimbaud's verse.

The square, with gravel paths and shabby lawns.
Correct, the trees and flowers repress their yawns.
The tradesman brings his favorite conceit,
To air it, while he stifles with the heat.

In the kiosk, the military band.
The shakos nod the time of the quadrilles.
The flaunting dandy strolls about the stand.
The notary, half unconscious of his seals.

This microcosm of Charleville that so captivated Rimbaud, Gray further recreates in his "Imitation" as he notes that

> On the green seats, small groups of grocermen,
> Absorbed, their sticks scooping a little hole
> Upon the path, talk market prices; then
> Take up a cue: I think, upon the whole...
>
> The loutish roughs are larking on the grass.
> The sentimental trooper, with a rose
> Between his teeth, seeing a baby, grows
> More tender, with an eye upon the nurse.

In the last three stanzas, Gray as translator is at his best. Noteworthy is his ability to keep the same movement and meaning of the original. To his credit, Gray not only constructed his phrases and arranged his stanzas exactly as Rimbaud did, but he also managed to reproduce Rimbaud's pattern of sound.

> Unbuttoned, like a student, I follow
> A couple of girls along the chestnut row.
> They know I am following, for they turn and laugh,
> Half impudent, half shy, inviting chaff.
>
> I do not say a word. I only stare
> At their round, fluffy necks. I follow where
> The shoulders drop; I struggle to define
> The subtle torso's hesitating line.
>
> Only my rustling tread, deliberate, slow;
> The rippled silence from the still leaves drips.
> They think I am an idiot, they speak low;
> —I feel faint kisses creeping on my lips.

As for Rimbaud's "Sensation," Gray translated this short poem skillfully, but its two quatrains read better in the original French than in Gray's "Imitation." The poem has none of the outrageous comparisons, grotesque rhymes, or sudden shifts in tone that Rimbaud loved to utilize. What it does have is a flood of lush imagery that concludes with the poet's desire "to go away / With nature, happily as a girl." This is one "Imitation" that has stirred little interest, though it did become a favorite with Olive Custance. She never explained why.[36]

Baudelaire

"A Une Madone" is an "Imitation" from Baudelaire that loses little of its well-planned structure in Gray's translation. Gray was drawn to this poem by its religious and erotic motifs, its continual switching of one set of feelings for another: from jealousy to respect, from respect to humility, from humility to adoration, from adoration to *volupté noire*. Not the least of the poem's attractiveness for Gray must have been the contrasts between Baudelaire's perverse feelings and his rich images. Fascinated by the erotomania and sado-masochism that jar against a religious setting, Gray nonetheless did soften some of the sensuality found in Baudelaire's poem, especially that which deals with physical desire and the hatred with which the serpent of jealousy stifles the spirit.

The poem that follows, "Femmes Damnees," is somewhat less effective than "A Une Madone."[37] Oozing with sensuousness, Baudelaire's damned women bring to mind the sadistic, lesbian "Dolores" and "Anactoria" of Swinburne. Swinburne knew "Femmes Damnees" well; it was one of the poems of Baudelaire he reviewed for the *Spectator* in 1862. Whether or not Swinburne knew Gray's translation of "Femmes Damnees" cannot be determined, but it is interesting to conjecture what he might have said about Gray's straining after effect, his attempt to capture the climacteric movement of a mood. Certainly he would have had a few favorable remarks about Gray's diction, which is filled with overtones of meaning. The poem, finally, is a potpourri of lush phrases, of patterns of sound and sense, not only found in Baudelaire but common among many of the other Symbolists as well.

"Voyage à Cythere" is the third "Imitation" from Baudelaire. The last poem in *Silverpoints*, it is also the longest. Bizarre as

"Voyage à Cythere" may initially seem, it is not one that the
"hypocrite lecteur" cannot easily forget; for the subject is an
imaginary voyage to Cythera, which turns out to be not the sexual
paradise of legend but a place of punishment and expiation for
sins of the flesh.

Close to the exact wording of the original, Gray begins the
voyage:

> Bird-like, my heart was glad to soar and vault;
> Fluttering among the cordages; and on
> The vessel flew, under an empty vault:
> An angel drunken of a radiant sun.
>
> Tell me, what is that gray, that sombre isle?
> 'Tis Cythera, famed on many a poet string;
> A name that has not lacked the slavering smile;
> But now, you see, it is not much to sing.

This Ionian isle consecrated to Venus, Gray describes, as Baudelaire did, not as an Eldorado but as a

> Sweet isle of myrtles, once of open blooms:
> Now only of lean lands most lean: it seems
> A flinty desert bitter with shrill screams:
> But one strange object on its horror looms.
>
> Not a fair temple, foiled with coppiced trees,
> Where the young priestess, mistress of the flowers,
> Goes opening her gown to the cool breeze,
> To still the fire, the torment that devours.

The voyage continues

> —as along the shore we skirted, near
> Enough to scare the birds with our white sails,
> We saw a three-limbed gibbet rising sheer,
> Detached against the sky in spare details.

Gray's rendition of Baudelaire's therapeutic descent into hell follows in stanzas that reflect the traditional dualism between the spiritual and the carnal, between aspirations toward purity and an equally intense inclination toward sensuality—aspiration and inclinations that had troubled Gray just as they had distressed Baudelaire.

> The eyes, two caves; and from the rotten paunch,
> Its freight, too heavy, streamed along the haunch.
> Hang for these harpies' hidden delight,
> Poor rag of flesh, torn of thy sex and sight!
>
> Cythera's child, child of so sweet a sky!
> Silent thou bearest insult—as we must—
> In expiation of what faults deny
> Thee even a shallow shelter in the dust.
>
> All thine isle showed me, Venus! was upthrust,
> A symbol calvary where my image hung.
> Give me, Lord God, to look upon that dung,
> My body and my heart, without disgust.

Gray must have recognized the effectiveness of his translation, his success in capturing the mood of deep depression and disgust that had so overwhelmed Baudelaire when he first composed the poem, a time when the author of *Les Fleurs du Mal* fell ill once more with a recurrence of the syphilis he had thought permanently cured.

Arthur Symons recognized the effectiveness of Gray's translation; and inspired by Gray's rendition, a few years later he too translated "Voyage à Cythère."[38] A comparison of Gray's translation with that of Symons has a special element of interest: the final couplet is the same in both versions. Since coincidence is highly improbable, it is not unreasonable to conclude, as Ruth Temple has remarked, that Symons "was persuaded of his inability to improve upon the earlier [Gray's] rendering."[39] And just as Symons recognized the effectiveness of Gray's translation, Gray also realized that "Voyage à Cythere" would be the proper coda to his volume. The last stanza of the poem, in particular, which is so startling in its intensity, tends to sum up the whole of Gray's *Silverpoints*.

A Postlude

At this point, all that could be said about *Silverpoints* has hardly been said; and even if it had, a supreme irony would still remain: Gray had serious regets about his early *poèmes noires*. In his later years, Gray did his utmost to locate and "immobilize" all existing copies of his first book of poetry. Moreover, he never allowed *Silverpoints* to be reprinted. Gordon Bottomly tried more than once to arrange a new edition, but Gray refused to give his consent. Individually, Gray reasoned, each one of the poems could stand on its own merits; taken collectively, he feared, they might be an occasion for scandal.

In 1928, Gray did grant permission to A. J. A. Symons to publish six poems from *Silverpoints*—"Mishka," "Crocuses in Grass," "Les Demoiselles de Sauve," "On a Picture," "Complaint," and "Lean Back, and Press the Pillow Deep"—in an anthology of nineties' verse. Four years later, he even extended permission to John Gawsworth to publish the two poems that Lane thought too daring to publish in *Silverpoints*—"Sound" and "Song of the Stars"; Gawsworth did so in his *Known Signatures*. In 1936, Yeats had hopes of including a few of the *Silverpoints* poems in his edition of the *Oxford Book of Modern Verse*, but he failed to obtain the necessary permission from Gray's literary executors. Two full years after Gray's death, there was still concern about scandal.

Over the years, many poems from *Silverpoints* have been selected for inclusion in various anthologies. And in 1973, a beautiful facsimile edition was issued by the Minerva Press of London. As though fearing profanation if Gray's icon of nineties' verse be offered to a general reading public, the Minerva Press limited *Silverpoints* to an edition of 250 copies—just as the Bodley Head had done eighty years before.

Chapter Four

Matters of the Spirit

The *Blue Calendars*

Shortly before Christmas 1894, Gray distributed the first of the *Blue Calendars* to close friends. A small blue-covered booklet measuring 4⅝ by 3⅜ inches, it contains twelve devotional poems assigned to the months of the forthcoming year. On the page following that of the title appear the words "A Book of Carols Invented and Writ by John Gray." Since the booklet was such a private affair, Gray noted the work was "Not for General Distribution," and also included his London address, "Forty-three Park Lane."

A second *Blue Calendar* appeared in 1895, a third in 1896, and a fourth in 1897. These three succeeding *Calendars* contained similar wording on the pages following their title pages, and each one of the four printings was limited to approximately one hundred copies. The very nature of the *Calendars* precluded their being sent to critics.

The first *Calendar* contains carols on the life of the Christ Child. Twelve sentimental prayerlike poems—one for each month of the year—are meant to make the mind and the heart receptive to matters of the spirit. With the words of Christ about becoming humble as little children uppermost in his mind, Gray composed these poems with a certain coyness and cloying charm. Ian Fletcher has aptly described this *Calendar* as "deliberately, elegantly whim-

77

sical; sophisticatedly naive...an attempt to regain the innocent ear and eye."[1]

One of the best of these poems of childlike joy and praise is that for May 1895:

> Good Saint Mary fumbled deep,
> With a saintly gesture.
> In this bag (said she) I keep
> All the Infant's vesture.
> Ah Lord! How great is my reward.
> My soul doth magnify the Lord.

The final line of this first stanza would of course be familiar to most of its readers, coming as it does from the opening line of the Magnificat, the canticle recited by Mary at the visitation to her cousin Elizabeth.

The fourth stanza reads:

> Here be little cambric shirts
> Very small and slender.
> Here the band His body girts,
> Which is frail and tender.
> So carefully must He be dressed.
> Henceforth all the nations call me blest.

The final line again echoes the Magnificat: "For behold henceforth all generations will call me blessed." The last line of each of the seven stanzas of this carol, in fact, comes from the Magnificat. Once the reader becomes aware of how cleverly Gray has structured this work, he is inclined to reread each stanza; and a rereading induces meditation upon the Magnificat, as Gray of course intended.

One grateful recipient of this first *Calendar* was Olive Custance, an attractive young poet whom Gray had met in 1891. Strongly drawn to him, she became one of his most enthusiastic admirers. She often consulted with Gray about her own poetry, even after she had made a reputation for herself in 1897 with the publication of her first volume, *Opals*.[2]

Flattered that he had sent her one of his *Calendars*, she recorded her appreciation in a short note that she wrote to a friend about her "Prince of Poets," as she referred to Gray, who "has lived a strange full life. . . ." In her less than objective judgment, there were few poets "who could sing like him—his poems are so precious and pure."[3]

Although most of the poems in the first *Calendar* that Olive Custance so admired might be labeled medieval in flavor, the poems that make up the second *Calendar* are more reminiscent of certain seventeenth-century religious works. Just as such metaphysical poets as George Herbert, Richard Crawshaw, and Thomas Traherne, for example, had juxtaposed pagan and Christian allusions in their devotional works, so did Gray.

A good example of Gray's blending of pagan and Christian imagery in the same work can be found in his poem for June 1896, "The True Vine." This poem, which is of course essentially devotional, takes its origin and title from Christ's messianic claim: "I am the true Vine, and my Father is the Vinedresser" (John 15:1). Throughout "The True Vine" Christ obviously is the vine, but many other references suggest Dionysus, and frequently the two blend into one.

> Another quells,
> Another reins the leopards.
> My portent tells
> My story to the shepherds
> Beside the wells.

> My face is tan.
> My hair, my hair is golden.
> None brighter than
> My eyes were e'er beholden
> By eyes of man.

> I am the vine.
> The cup is chiseled garnet
> For garnet wine.

I am the vine incarnate.
          The grape is mine.

     With crown of bright
Green leaf and tender clusters
          My head is dight;
Even as the starry musters
          Adorn the night.

     I am the vine:
The stock, the grape, the dresser;
          In deed and sign,
The purple-footed presser
          Of purple wine.

Gray's knowledge of the classics and of the imagery of the metaphysical poets of the seventeenth century allowed him to utilize Dionysus as a proto-Christ figure. All sorts of religious rites, he knew, had been associated with the pagan divinity of Dionysus, the god who introduced the culture of the vine and the making of wine. Dionysus, being more than a simple god of revelry, symbolically prefigures Christ. Dionysus was the god of wine; Christ used wine at the Last Supper; and every priest of the Roman Church is held by Catholics to transubstantiate wine at mass.

In Gray's poem, it is Dionysus who "quells . . . reins the leopards" that pull his chariot, the divinity that first cultivated the vine; but it is Christ, the Good Shepherd, who is "the stock, the grape," indeed "the vine incarnate." The dionysian joy of Christ as Priest and Victim that Gray manages in "The True Vine" especially appealed to Dowson; but then, he was enthusiastic about the entire second *Calendar*. On December 27, 1895, he penned a short letter of appreciation. "I can't tell you how delighted I am with the *Calendar*," he informed Gray. "It is something quite apart, rare, audacious, successful—admirable in a word."[4]

Each *Calendar* that Gray distributed to his friends elicited favorable response. Beardsley, for one, was quite pleased with the third *Calendar.* In a letter to Raffalovich written on December 12, 1896, he remarked "what a charming little Calendar Gray has sent forth."[5] This third *Calendar*, like the fourth which followed in 1897, consists of sonnets addressed to various saints. Several of these sonnets are technically perfect. The sonnets in *The Fourth and Last Blue Calendar*, as Gray entitled the *Calendar* for 1898, are even better. The one for January addressed to St. Agnes and another for October addressed to St. Teresa are among the best of all Gray's sonnets.

Lady Gregory did not comment upon the sonnets as sonnets, but apparently she was so pleased with each of the *Calendars* that she had them bound together in a dark green calfskin cover. The work, exquisitely bound, has the appearance of a small prayer book, and its well-thumbed appearance allows the inference that it was so used.[6] Had Lady Gregory read through her little book of devotional poems critically she might have observed that the sonnets in the third and fourth *Calendars* are less didactic and more evocative than the poems found in the first and second *Calendars.*

Judging from the way Lady Gregory read all four *Calendars*, they served their purpose well; still, it might be objected that several carols and sonnets, being more in the nature of devotional verse, are aesthetically deficient. Good religious poetry, Gray himself would have been the first to admit, requires some manifestation of the bitter-sweet conflicts between God and the soul of the poet. Writing his four *Calendars* served a purpose for Gray, but he did not attempt a fifth.

What he accomplished is worthy of commendation; to render an overall judgment is difficult. As every serious reader of religious poetry is well aware, the poet who creates in this genre has not only the task of struggling with suitable imagery but, additionally, excessive spirituality often seems to diminish poetic expression. Several of the poems in the *Calendars*, nonetheless, are quite effective, especially "Good St. Mary" (May 1895) and "The True Vine" (June 1896).

Anyone who reads through Gray's *Calendars* is bound to discover several works that will appeal to him. Ian Fletcher, for example, thinks highly of certain sonnets in the third and fourth *Calendars*, in particular the one for November 1897 addressed to the Spanish mystic, St. John of the Cross:

> Praise to thee, gentle friar, John of the Cross!
> The body was the only living thing
> Whereon thou hadst not pity: thou didst wring
> Its frailty till it knew not thorns from moss.
>
> Above where this mean world's vexations toss,
> Thou art a flame on Carmel; thou'st a wing
> Thyself of contemplation; thou dost fling
> All pediments aside; thy wealth a loss.
>
> Thine ecstacy demands the utmost night,
> Wherein to espy the Lover's glimmering light;
> Thy dearest hope abandonment of men,
>
> Whereby to know the beauty beyond ken.
> Sweet lilies mark the desert thou hast trod.
> The steep of Carmel traced thy path to God.

What Fletcher likes most about this sonnet, which he has labeled "superbly baroque," is the quick mutation of the saint from a flame into a wing, and then into "a violent architecture of contemplation, together with the lean authority of statements such as 'Thine ecstasy demands the utmost night.'"[7] But when Fletcher goes on to extol "St. John of the Cross" and other sonnets in the third and fourth *Calendars* as not too far below those of Gerard Manley Hopkins, he goes a bit too far. To carp about his judgment would be unwarranted; nevertheless, though Gray may have been occasionally Hopkinsesque, his *Calendars* are not quite on a par with the best of Hopkins's work. The dictional and metrical experimentation of both poets, neither of whom was aware of the prosodic pursuits of the other, is not without interest, however.

Osbert Burdett was one of the first critics to link the names of

Gray and Hopkins. Not wholly appreciative of Gray's "rendering halts," Burdett tended to dismiss the author of the *Calendars* as a poet "who can write but cannot sing."[8] Gray's original verses, like those of Hopkins, Burdett observed, "seem to shun a smooth rhythm...Indeed, the sense is apt to be at the mercy of Gray's interlaced little meters."[9] Gray was, as Burdette read him, a delicate if imitative poet, an accomplished craftsman, a forerunner of contemporary poetry, a true innovator—but one who could not quite approach either the technicalities or final accomplishments of Gerard Manley Hopkins.

In a limited sense, Gray's *Calendars* contain his assured meditations. They are made up of poems of a strictly private nature, as many of the recipients of the *Calendars* were well aware. Gray had let his close friends know, directly and indirectly, that he was concentrating his creativity on a volume of religious poetry that would serve as a corrective of sorts to the secularity of *Silverpoints.* In one of his letters to Gray, for example, Dowson indicates that he knew that Gray was working on just such a volume of devotional poetry. On December 27, 1895, he wrote that he was looking forward to Gray's new hymns "with an increased anticipation. . . ."[10] The collection of Gray's new hymns would be entitled *Spiritual Poems.*

Spiritual Poems

In 1896, two years before Gray left London for Rome to prepare himself for the Roman Catholic priesthood, he published his first full-scale volume of religious poetry, *Spiritual Poems.* Like *Silverpoints, Spiritual Poems* is a beautifully designed volume. Once again, Gray was fortunate in having Charles Ricketts lay out the book.

Although not as physically impressive as *Silverpoints*, this work conforms to Ricketts's demands for "total art." Approximately eight by five inches in size, *Spiritual Poems* is bound in light gray paper boards. In the upper right-hand corner of its cover is a white label. Within the label the title is printed in black and ornamented with an oxeye daisy. To further distinguish his work, Ricketts prepared a wood-engraved frontispiece and border. Next he designed a typography appropriate for an exquisite white paper. And then he personally supervised a limited run of 210 copies at the Ballantyne Press in London.

The volume contains a total of forty poems. Eleven are original, twenty-nine, translations. The original poems, which are addressed to the Holy Trinity, Christ, the Blessed Mother, St. Joseph, St. Sebastian, and other saints, are expressive of Gray's devotion. The translated works come from a wide range of writers, Catholic and Protestant, and from Latin, French, Spanish, and German poems; they include such emblem poets as Alonso de Ledesma and such little known liturgical poets as B. Notker, the Monk of St. Gall. Both the translations and the originals are indicative of Gray's religious zeal and are reflective of the variety and extent of his spiritual reading. Several of the translated works, moreover, suggest that Gray was fascinated by those ecstatic moments of mystical union with Christ on the part of various saints that he had read about.

Aware that one of his original poems, "The Tree of Knowledge," had considerable merit, Gray placed it in prime position. Embedded on the title page within the elaborate design of Ricketts's frontispiece, its opening lines recommend that the Tree of Knowledge required a Cross of Salvation:

> From what meet jewel seed
>   Did the tree spring?
> How first beat its new life in bleak abode
> Of virgin rock, strange metals for its food,
> Toward its last hewn mould, the bitter rood?
> First did it sprout, indeed,
>   A double wing?

In utilizing the traditional image of the Tree as the instrument of both man's fall and regeneration, Gray achieved a commendable directness through a simplicity of diction and a complexity of extended imagery. In addition, although the poet remains the speaker in the twelve stanzas that follow, the point of view is that of the Tree:

> Mine 'tis, of fruit mine own,
>   To work this deed:
> Earnest of promise absolute, these green
> Sweet wings; a million engines pulse therein,
> Yet can I leave not a space, to lean
>   Upon a fulcrum known,
>   To know my need.

Endowed as the Tree is with sensitivity, humility, and sympathy, it is reminiscent of the Anglo-Saxon "Dream of the Rood." Gray's Tree of Knowledge, however, knowing of the creation of "Insect and fowl and beast / And sons of the earth," has a realization of hope. But the Tree laments deeply over the forbidden fruit eaten by the "gardener" and his "spouse."

Consequently, upon the fall of Adam and Eve, all the sons of earth have to be redeemed by God the Son; for as mankind goes forth and multiplies, there follows "Race upon savage race, / Rough brood on brood." Always cognizant of the Tree, the progeny of our First Parents hate its very shape. Sorely they refashion it into a cross. In its new form, the Tree realized that only in "yon athlete, stripped for my embrace" is there someone who "knows about it all. / He knows, he knows."

In the reality of the Cross of Calvary, the Tree and Christ achieve a unity. The final stanza, with its stress on the emotions of sorrow and love, distills the thought that out of the Tree of Knowledge came both the fall of man and his eventual redemption.

One of the more memorable of the *Spiritual Poems* is "St. Sebastian. On a Picture." In this impassioned work, as its title indicates, Gray delineates upon a painting of the saint at his martyrdom. What specific painting Gray had in mind, if not a composite of his own mental creation, is difficult to determine.

Having a fondness for St. Sebastian,[11] who is invariably depicted in art as a beautiful, well-formed youth either dreamily indifferent to or masochistically ecstatic about the arrows that penetrate his thinly clad and bloodied body, Gray collected several paintings of this rather passive saint. Then, again, he was always on the lookout for others, as can be determined from several references to St. Sebastian in letters of Beardsley written to Gray and Raffalovich.[12] Through the kindness of Beardsley, Gray obtained a reproduction of Callot's "St. Sebastian" and another by Pinturricchio.

In his poem, Gray depicts the martyrdom of one of his favorite saints entirely in the present tense through a series of elaborate descriptions. Foremost is a downward staircase, with each descending step designated as being "ever mauver than its fellow mauve." Gray goes on to convey the emotions of others looking helplessly on the torment of Sebastian "in a hush so still. / The stair they stand on scarcely knows the throes / Of their unanimous breathing."

The backdrop is a landscape

> . . . where an orange grove
> Has all the seeming of a labyrinth,
> Even as orange as the heaven is mauve;
> The sun is gold as heaven is mauve;
> The sun is gold as heaven is hyacinth,
> As glowing as a founder's open stove.

At the right there is "an insolent pavilion" with "lilac clusters" heavily drooping against tent walls. The reader's attention is then shifted from the mauve heaven and orange earth to a vision of an inferno where "knotty limbs are fierce with scarlet stuff" and "rank hair veils . . . ears, which harken not." Next there is the military captain, the executioner, wearing "the reddest hose / Impatient, armed, and legs akimbo / Aiming, with one clinched eye and wrinkled nose," ready to fire his darts.

Rapid trochaics now describe the saint as filled with love and dripping blood. Recoiling from the role of martyr he is being forced to play, his feet "Clutch the ground for strength." But at last, his eyes

> ... reluctant turn
> From the wicket crew;
> Eyes with love which burn
> For the ill they do,
> Heavenward must turn.

The thirteenth and final stanza once more emphasizes Sebastian's humanity. His skin "Cannot choose but shrink." Though his eyes are fixed on heaven, his feet firmly embrace the ground. "Shamed because of sin," he has had, apparently, a harrowing vision of hell. Poised between the diabolical and the divine, he draws his last human breath. The livid spectators to his grisly death await "The holy hour" when with "more than earthly night shall night be dark."

"St. Sebastian. On a Picture" of *Spiritual Poems* has much in common with "On a Picture" of *Silverpoints.* When Gray wrote "On a Picture," his subject was the death of the beautiful Ophelia; but this poem on a picture about the tragic heroine of one of Shakespeare's plays is reflective of Gray's own Hamlet-like preoccupation with the weighty problem of existence. "On a Picture" allows the inference that Gray, like another Ophelia, desired to unburden himself of all earthly care. "St. Sebastian" also allows the inference that Gray was, literally, troubled by "the slings and arrows of outrageous fortune"; but if suffering and death are inevitable, then at least he, like another Sebastian, could die a witness to Christ. To the sensitive Hamlet lingering outside a picture of Ophelia, life and death had little meaning. To the sensitive Gray contemplating the painting of the martyrdom of St. Sebastian, art and beauty could transform existence—provided religious faith were the catalytic agent.

Gray's full acceptance of his religious faith is evident in most of the *Spiritual Poems*, particularly in "To the Blessed Virgin." In contrast to the vibrant intensity of "St. Sebastian," this hymn to the Virgin is marked by a radiant serenity. The opening lines are a litany to Mary, wherein she is addressed as "Gate of Crystal," "Medicine of Desolation," "Thornless Blossom of Salvation."

But Gray is not guilty of Mariolatry. The emphasis is upon the birth of her Divine Son:

> Wonderful, a thing unknown;
> Lo, a maid conceiving;
> God is clothed in flesh and bone;
> Marvel past believing.

The doctrines of the Virgin Birth and the Incarnation are amplified in lines that follow. Christ is petitioned as "Son of Heaven and star of earth," the son of "a damsel mother." As for his actual birth, it is described as one in which

> Though a thousand sunrays pass
> Through a fastened casement,
> Nothing ill befalls the glass,
> Wreakage or abasement.

The sunlight image is continued—"Thus, and subtler than the sun"—and gradually is made to merge with divine light:

> Eyes accessible to ours,
> Keep the light which dowered.
> Gay the garden bore its flowers,
> Mother undeflowered.

The poem concludes with this pointed reference to Mary's perpetual virginity and a final prayer to the damsel mother, "Whiter than the lily is, / Like the roses prolific," to "Ask thy son's indulgencies, / Virgin beatific."

"Lord, if Thou Art Not Present" is less of a prayer and paean of praise than "To the Blessed Virgin" and more of an attempt to describe the union of a mystic with Christ. Midway through this poem, the speaker states his own complete dependence upon his limited knowledge of God:

> Unless Thou teach
> Me, Lord I cannot seek; nor can I find
> Thee, if Thou wilt not come within my reach.

Though much of what Gray has to say in this poem is not uncommon in devotional verse, his diction imparts a complex variety of nuances to his theme. Especially significant is his use of terza rima to control the exuberance of his thought. The work concludes, appropriately, with an assertion that through desire and love man may seek and eventually merit his salvation.

A companion poem, "They say, In Other Days," also has for its theme the mystic's desire for union with Christ. Mainly because of its lengthened development, this is a more polished work of poetic art; its sixty-two lines are far more successful than the thirteen lines of "Lord, If Thou Art Not Present."

Essentially, the narrative of "They Say, In Other Days" concerns the journey of the soul of St. John of the Cross. Once in heaven, his soul becomes "folded in the hands of Christ." The nail wounds in Christ's hands inform the saint of the darkness that envelops all men, that because of the "blindness" of his own nature could John come to experience the dark night of the soul. The spear wound in Christ's side further informs the saint that "I ached for this dear hour, my darling one. / Thou wert a proper vessel for the Wine / I gave thee to dispense." Toward the end of the poem, the Sacred Heart cradles the saint, and the work concludes with the complete desire of the saint to be so encradled.

There is nothing that is personal in "They Say, In Other Days," but the autobiographical nature of several of the *Spiritual Poems* is discernible in those concerned with the theme of repentance. "The Two Sinners," for example, is a duologue between a Godfrey and an Oliver. Behind the personae, it is reasonable to infer, stand Raffalovich and Gray respectively. In an agonizing sense of sinfulness, each one utters a prayer of contrition in a kind of musical duet.

The dialogue of Godfrey and Oliver continues in another poem, "Repentance." Here, an opening question of G: "Is it his mercy or his judgement rod?" is answered by O: "Repentance is an un-sought gift of God." Four more couplets have the speakers in their repentance humbly seek solace with the Crucified Christ.

> O: Hath he not borne our griefs and with them this?
> G: If we accept it not, we do amiss.
> O: One way, repentance, leads to life,
>   he saith Who lieth not.
> G: All others lead to death.
> O: It is a grace; and faith and life are kin.
> G: He saith not it shall always follow sin.
> O: Then God have mercy on us, feeble men;
>   and brings us to himself.
> G: Amen.

One of the finest translations in *Spiritual Poems* is that of the "Oscura Noche" of St. John of the Cross. Gray had a special interest in this sixteenth-century Spanish saint, cofounder with St. Teresa of Avila of the Discalced Carmelites. A mystic, St. John of the Cross had written two treatises on the attainment of spiritual perfection, *The Ascent of Mount Carmel* and *The Dark Night of the Soul*, works that Gray found fascinating. He was especially taken up with St. John of the Cross's central thesis: the soul, con-sisting of both sensual and spiritual parts, must be cleansed of all imperfections before it can attain union with the All-Perfect.

The purgation of the soul, Gray learned from reading St. John of the Cross, could be likened to a dark night into which the soul must be plunged in order that the Divine Light may take up its abode within this darkness. The dark night, furthermore, takes place when the soul, through meditation and cooperation with habitual grace, empties itself of all impurities and creature attachments and allows God to act upon and take possession of it.

In "Oscura Noche," the dark night is a symbol of the saint's mystical experience within the period of his ultimate purification, an experience exceedingly difficult to verbalize. To translate St. John's concepts effectively, it was virtually a prerequisite that Gray have an understanding of mystical contemplation, prayer that is essentially passive, and an appreciation of the direct action of God on the soul.

Gray had been drawn to St. John of the Cross because he too had undergone mystical experiences of a sort; he, too, had experienced the sensual and aspired to the spiritual. He would have been quick to deny that he ever had the rare perceptions of the true mystic, but he did undergo his own "Dark Night of the Soul." There was no "darker" period in his life than when, shortly after the publication of *Silverpoints* in 1893, he actually inclined toward suicide. But a purgation of sorts occurred when he broke with Wilde the following year and underwent a second and lasting conversion. And it was about the time of Beardsley's death in 1898 that he experienced an illumination and decided to enter the priesthood.

Having gone through his own dark night, Gray found St. John's poem all the more meaningful. To say that his translation equals, if not surpasses, other renditions of St. John's remarkable poem from Spanish into English is not an exaggeration. The excellence of Gray's translation becomes self-evident when compared with some of the better known versions of Roy Campbell, John Frederick Nims, and Edgar Allison Peers.[13] Especially noteworthy is Gray's use of St. John's five-line stanza and individualized rhyme scheme, down to the end rhyme of the second line of each stanza that serves to link successive stanzas.

I

> Once in the senses' night,
> Obscure the night, with anxious passion burning
> (O happy hour of flight!)
> Forth unobserved I crept;
> For all my house lay sunk in rest, and slept.

II

> Secure in covering night,
> Disguised, by secret stairways, none discerning;
> (O happy hour of flight!)
> Forth unobserved I crept;
> For all my house lay sunk in rest, and slept.

In the five stanzas that follow, Gray symbolizes "the dark night's wing" unilluminated by "lantern" or "guide." But the darkness becomes "more lovely than the dawn" when the night unites "The lover with the loved; / And changed into the lover the beloved!" Throughout the long night God did "rest" while the mystic "entertained," until

VIII

> Fainting and all distraught;
> My drooping head was resting on my love;
> Senseless, resisting not,
> I cast off all my cares,
> Fallen among sweet lillies unawares.

Spiritual Poems was published at a time when Gray had his mind on matters of the spirit rather than aspects of literature. He did little, consequently, to call his new volume of poetry to the attention of others who might not be especially responsive to religious poetry. He had sent *Silverpoints* out for impersonal review; *Spiritual Poems* was more in the nature of a personal expression.

And so Gray was not particularly concerned about what literary critics might have to say about his devotional poetry. He was concerned about the edification of his close friends, however, and he made certain therefore to send them copies.

Dowson recorded his reception of *Spiritual Poems* in a letter he wrote to Arthur Symons on July 5, 1896. Though Dowson failed to speak critically of the volume, he did note that Gray's mysticism seemed sincere.[14] Others may have suspected that Gray's devotional poetry was just another literary display, another subject for him to write about, but Dowson was properly perceptive about his friend's religious zeal.

Beardsley, too, was impressed with Gray's *Spiritual Poems.* On July 6, he wrote Leonard Smithers, who was then publishing the *Savoy,* an avant-garde journal of which Beardsley was art editor: "Gray has just sent me a copy of his new book of verses. They are *really admirable* and might be reviewed . . . in our monthly. I wish

Gray was asked more frequently to contribute for us, he is one of the few younger men worth printing."[15] But Beardsley's suggestion to Smithers did not produce a review. The demise of the *Savoy* was at hand. A few months later, the journal ceased publication with its December issue, having struggled through eight issues.

There are other references to *Spiritual Poems* in Beardsley's letters that demonstrate his high regard for the work. On October 22, 1897, for example, he wrote Smithers from Paris to sell most of his books. Beardsley had several large debts to discharge. He instructed Smithers to keep only four books, one of them *Spiritual Poems*.[16] A few months later, on February 4, 1898, after having discovered that Gray's volume had inadvertently been consigned for sale, he again wrote Smithers. "Please don't sell *Spiritual Poems*," he implored. Though he also complained about having to "linger in bed," he added: "The *Spiritual Poems* you might get Zaensdorff or someone to put into a scarlet maroquin cover for me."[17]

A few copies of *Spiritual Poems* had been directed to friends in Paris. Although hardly as exuberant in their praise as Beardsley, they too thought highly of the work. Huysmans, for one, recorded his reaction to Gray's religious verse in a letter he directed to Raffalovich. The author of *En Route* commented that he found Gray's devotional works quite interesting, and he even went so far as to draw a favorable contrast between Gray's efforts in a most demanding genre with what was being written in France, "where religious poetry consists only of low canticles."[18]

Contemporary critics have had little to say about Gray's *Spiritual Poems*. Reasons for neglect are not difficult to find. Foremost, Gray's devotional verse has had such a limited number of readers. Several poems from *Silverpoints* have appeared in various anthologies of nineties' verse, but with the exception of "The Tree of Knowledge," "On the Holy Trinity," and "Lord, If Thou Art Not Present," no other *Spiritual Poems* have been republished.[19] When *Spiritual Poems* is mentioned today by a critic, the volume is invariably contrasted with *Silverpoints*, and the former immediately adjudged less worthy of attention than the latter.

Then, too, critics often have a tendency to echo one another.

If specialists in Gray's poetry speak of *Spiritual Poems* in a cursory fashion, other critics are hardly going to be encouraged to evaluate the volume on their own. Ian Fletcher, for example, looks upon *Spiritual Poems* as a work of diminished success that forms "a devotional 'imaginary museum' and reflects the self-conscious eclecticism of the 90's, with its memory of Pater's 'all periods, types, schools of taste, are in themselves equal.' "[20]

Finally, *Spiritual Poems* has aroused little attention for the simple reason that there is no great interest in devotional poetry, on the part of either the dedicated critic or the general reader.[21] The religious works of such poets as John Donne, George Herbert, Richard Crashaw, and other "metaphysicals" may command some attention, but even the poems of these well-known seventeenth-century figures are read today more as examples of compelling literature than as works of spiritual devotion.

The Last Letters of Aubrey Beardsley

Gray first met Aubrey Beardsley early in the nineties at a time when they both had achieved initial success, Gray with his *Silverpoints* and Beardsley with his appointment as art editor of the *Yellow Book*. Over the next few years, they met many times, enjoyed each other's company, and became reasonably close friends.

Gray especially admired Beardsley's illustrations for Malory's *Morte d'Arthur* and Pope's *Rape of the Lock*; about some of the artist's daring and rather indelicate posters, Gray had his reservations. Beardsley, on his part, admired most of Gray's poetry and often told him so. He reacted enthusiastically to Gray's *Silverpoints*, his *Blue Calendars*, and his *Spiritual Poems*. Beardsley also liked *The Ambush of Young Days* and *The Northern Aspect*, which he had seen at a private performance in Raffalovich's London home. In an undated letter he wrote to Gray sometime during May 1896, he offered to illustrate *The Northern Aspect*.[22]

Many of Beardsley's letters written during 1895 and 1896 contain warm references to Gray and his poetry,[23] but the more important letters, as far as Gray was concerned, were those his artist friend wrote to him and Raffalovich during 1897 and 1898. Beardsley did not attach much importance to these letters written during the last two years of his short life; but a few years after his death on March 16, 1898, Gray decided to publish these last letters he and Raffalovich had received from the artist. He had several good reasons for doing so.

Gray believed that a volume he planned to entitle simply *The Last Letters of Aubrey Beardsley* would put his late friend's life into better perspective, that the more perceptive reader would recognize that in Beardsley's case his ill health was a kind of thurible in which the dross of a brief and tainted life burned away. In short, such a book would be more than a tribute to Beardsley, for Gray hoped that the last letters written by the artist might correct the popular view of Beardsley's being a kind of Fra Angelico of Satanism.

Gray, therefore, prepared the letters he had collected with a care bordering on reverence. And since Beardsley's mother was in financial need, Gray made special arrangements with his publisher, Longmans Green and Company. "I propose," he noted in a letter dated October 1, 1904, "to hand all proceeds of royalties to his mother, to dispose of as she thinks fit."[24]

The charge that Gray maneuvered a sick and confused Beardsley to convert to the Church of Rome, and that it was done with the leverage of Raffalovich's money, is still frequently heard.[25] To counter such canards, one Beardsley scholar recently commented that it is pure nonsense to suggest that Beardsley was dragged "sneering and blaspheming across some vast divide; that it was a need to keep him in with his paymaster that did the trick."[26] This same scholar, furthermore, sees no incompatibility between Beardsley's backsliding and belief: "The more heinous the sin, the more desperate may be the sinner's sense of the punishing presence of God."[27]

Although it is true that Raffalovich supplied Beardsley with funds after his dismissal from the *Yellow Book*, that he supported the destitute artist with a regular allowance from February 1897 to his death some thirteen months later, Raffalovich rendered financial aid mainly out of friendship and a high regard for Beardsley. It was Beardsley who first turned to Raffalovich for help. He knew that Raffalovich had helped other struggling artists and impoverished friends. Raffalovich had not bribed others nor would he bribe Beardsley to convert to the Roman Church.

In the case of Gray, it was the artist's deathbed conversion that precipitated Gray's decision to give himself wholly to the church, to seek ordination, not the other way round. To suggest that Gray hovered over the dying Beardsley and pressured him to convert is to ignore some basic facts.

Foremost is Beardsley's own spiritual nature. All his life he felt the need of the protective stability that religion alone can offer. Even in his youth, he had a fascination for the supernatural. As an artist, he had a special appreciation for religious ritual. He believed, moreover, that he once beheld a vision of a bleeding Christ, an experience he related to such intimates as Symons and Yeats.[28] Then, too, he had the example of his sister Mabel, who converted to the Church of Rome a full year before he did. That both Mabel and Aubrey were sincere in their adopted faith can be inferred from the example they gave their parents, who also sought refuge in Roman Catholicism.

When Beardsley did convert early in 1897, the news spread quickly among his friends and acquaintances. Some were happy to learn that he had found a spiritual means of dealing with his physical deterioration. Others doubted his sincerity. A few openly scoffed. Gray, however, knew that Beardsley's turning to Rome was more than a passing whim, that it had come about through a proper spiritual impulse. Beardsley's last letters demonstrate, if anything, his complete sincerity.

In one such letter to Raffalovich, dated April 1, 1897, for example, Beardsley analyzes his mental state at the time of his conversion. "I feel now, dear André," he wrote, "like someone who has been standing waiting on the doorstep of a house upon a cold day, and who cannot make up his mind to knock for a long while. At last the door is thrown open and all the warmth of kind hospitality makes glad the frozen traveller."[29] And then in the dozens of letters to Raffalovich and Gray that followed with regularity, Beardsley wrote zealously of his devotional reading, prayer, the mass, the Eucharist. After his conversion, Beardsley headed each of his letters to Raffalovich with the salutation "My dearest Brother" [in Christ], those to Gray, "My dear Gray."

As editor of the letters, Gray took care to arrive at a proper chronological arrangement, rendered difficult by Beardsley's indifference to dating and the loss of postmarked envelopes in many cases. Where necessary, Gray supplied explanatory footnotes. He felt it obligatory to suppress certain passages that might cause pain or displeasure to others. For similar reasons, in some cases he used arbitrary signs for proper names that had been mentioned in less than favorable light. In most cases, though, the letters are in their original form, even faults of orthography and slips of the pen not being altered.

The names of the recipients are not given. Most of the letters had been addressed to Raffalovich, others to Gray. Neither wanted his name used. Raffalovich did not want it generally known that he had done all that could have been done to alleviate Beardsley's financial plight. Nor did Gray want the slightest commendation for any spiritual comfort he may have given the stricken artist.

At first, Gray was troubled by a recommendation from Longmans Green that he delete some details in the correspondence that focused on the horrors of consumption. "We are strongly of the opinion," he responded early in October of 1904, "that whatever there is of horror is vital to the interest of the letters, inasmuch as it serves to exhibit the moral victory of the sufferer and the power of divine grace in him."[30] But after writing this letter to Longmans Green, he reconsidered the objectionable aspect of some of the health details that Beardsley himself had noted in his letters. In a letter to Raffalovich of October 6, he discoursed on his qualms. Concerned about what insensitive critics might say about the book, Gray concluded that it might be well to excise here and there in order "to prevent some idiot from calling the book 250 pages of ghoulish gloating over the sufferings of a consumptive boy."[31]

Gray was correct in suspecting that the *Last Letters* might be misunderstood. Typical of a few adverse responses is that of Robert Ross, a friend of Beardsley and his family, an intimate in the Wilde circle, and editor of Wilde's *Complete Works* (1921). In his study of Beardsley, Ross wrote: "I do not doubt Beardsley's sincerity in the religion he embraced, but his expression of it in his letters. At least, I hope it was insincere. The letters left on some of us a disagreeable impression...."[32]

Ross, it appears, reacted negatively to Beardsley's display of piety in his letters. "A fescennine temperament is too often aligned with religiosity," Ross complained,[33] ignorant of or conveniently forgetting that Beardsley during the final days of his life begged that all his bawdy drawings be destroyed. It is difficult to believe that Ross did not know of the last letter Beardsley wrote to Smithers, in which the dying artist implored Smithers "to destroy *all* copies of Lysistrata and bad drawings...By all that is holy all obscene drawings." Beardsley's letter, which is postmarked March 7, 1898, contains a further plea in a postscript: "In my death agony."[34]

In taking the stand that Ross did, he was guilty of unconscious jealousy. He resented the benevolence that Gray and Raffalovich had directed toward Beardsley, a benevolence that he could never equal. Whatever his motives may have been, Ross further lamented that far more interesting than the letters that Gray published would have been the correspondence that Beardsley carried on with the writer Joseph Pennell, "one of the saner influences; or those [letters] to Aubrey Beardsley's mother and sister."[35] Once more, however, Ross was ignorant of or conveniently forgot the facts that Beardsley never carried on a correspondence with Pennell and that Aubrey's mother and sister saved virtually none of the letters he ever wrote them.

In an attempt to divert such uncalled-for criticism as that which Ross so ungraciously displayed, Gray wrote a long introduction to his collection of Beardsley's letters to clarify certain matters. First, he stressed Beardsley's personal qualities: "He was utterly devoid of any malevolence towards his fellow creatures, whether individually or collectively.... Not even the sternest of his critics will deny his sincerity or his sobriety, but such an outspoken man as he was with incorrigible youthfulness of spirit will sometimes shock the anxious and arouse the suspicion that he is perpetrating a malicious mystification."[36]

Had Beardsley lived, Gray went on to emphasize, "he might have risen, whether through his art or otherwise, spiritually to a height from which he could command the horizon he was created to scan. As it was, the long anguish, the increasing bodily helplessness, the extreme necessity in which someone else raises one's hand, turns one's head, showed the slowly-dying man things he had not seen before. He came face to face with the old riddle of life and death; the accustomed supports and resources of his being removed; his soul, thus denuded, discovered needs that unstable desires had hitherto obscured...."[37]

The 180 letters, which are plainly written without pose or self-pity, form a diary of Beardsley's last two years of life. They cover, specifically, a period before his conversion to a little less than three weeks before his death in 1898. They focus on a time when he hung on to his mortal existence with the unreasonable optimism of the consumptive frightfully aware of the nature and course of his malady. Like another Keats, Beardsley knew that mortality weighed heavily upon him; and like the last letters of Keats, these last letters of Beardsley are intense, absorbed, unflinching.

When the artist was only twenty-four, he first learned of the gravity of his condition. As he noted in a letter of June 5, 1896, his physician "pronounced very unfavorably on my condition to-day."[38] Early the following year, it was apparent that he was not going to live much longer. Gray and Raffalovich made a journey to Bournemouth to visit their ailing friend. At Raffalovich's expense, Beardsley traveled to London and from there to Paris. Once again, toward the end of April, Gray and Raffalovich made a visit to their dying friend.

Several months later, when Beardsley had actually gotten as far as the south of France on what proved to be his funeral journey, he was buoyed with expectations of a complete recovery. Shortly after, however, his condition grew worse. The frequency and severity of hemorrhages alarmed him. One severe attack followed another.

Toward the end of February 1898 he wrote his final letter. From then on, he was too weak to hold a pen. On March 16, cognizant of his untimely end, he died, a rosary clasped in his frail, wasted hands. Back in England, Beardsley's death was covered in newspapers and periodicals. Most journalists commented on his great talent, on his sensational drawings, on his editing of the *Yellow Book*. They tended to ignore his saintly death and to write of him mainly as a diabolic influence on British art. To controvert such viewpoints, Gray in a brief epilogue to his edition of Beardsley's letters, noted that there was a funeral mass said for Beardsley at the Cathedral of Menton on March 17.

Everything was tragic yet beautiful: "The dear heart himself would have loved it. There was music. The road from the Cathedral to the Cemetery was so wonderfully beautiful, winding up a hill; it was long and steep as we walked. His grave is on the edge of the hill; it is hewn out of the rock, and is a true sepulchre, with an arched opening and a stone closing it. We thought of the sepulchre of the Lord...."[39]

In reading through Beardsley's last letters, as Arthur Symons once lamented, "we see a man die."[40] And yet, one can also discover a measure of hope in his suffering. His hunger for life may be counterbalanced by the fear that possessed him when he became tabescent during the final weeks, but his letters are, as they were once described, "still full of a sweetness which is heroic in so passionate a life."[41]

The world of art that Beardsley created survives with undiminished brilliance. Today his work is very much in vogue—both for itself and for the major and potent influence it has had upon modern art. His last letters, while hardly so well known, may be just as important as his art. Perhaps it is not really too much of an exaggeration to claim, as one critic has done, that "the most poignant legacy Beardsley bequeathed to the world does not lie in his innumerable drawings, but in that collection of letters addressed to his friend...John Gray."[42]

Chapter Five

Creative Once More

Abreast of Modern Literature

After Gray edited and published *The Last Letters of Aubrey Beardsley* in 1904, he wrote and published little else for some twenty years. Reasons for his abandonment of literature are not hard to find. One was his vocation of parish priest. Parochial duties, liturgical services, baptisms, confessions, weddings, and funerals claimed a great deal of his time and absorbed much of his energy. At his ordination he had solemnly promised to place his life at the service of his church. His first twenty years in Edinburgh demonstrate that he fulfilled that vow.

A more significant reason for Gray's abandonment of literature may be found in a certain self-abasement to which he subjected himself. In drawing the curtain down on his past, he had virtually convinced himself that all he had written as a young poet was trivial and empty; but now, after almost twenty years of aesthetic repression, Gray once more found his voice. The artist in him had been stilled long enough.

In 1922, he broke his self-imposed silence with a series of poems and essays that he began to contribute to *Blackfriars*, a Dominican review of religious and political affairs, of literature and art. Since he was a Tertiary in the Dominican Order,[1] and frequently mixed with Dominican friars, the pages of their journal were open to him.

Gray may have entertained self-doubts and even thought of himself at times as an ex-poet, but the Dominicans, who knew of Gray's literary background, felt that virtually anything he might contribute to *Blackfriars* would enhance the reputation of their publication. Nor were they alone in their high opinion of Gray's literary ability and their belief that Gray was anxious to write again. A good number of writers and poets with whom Gray had corresponded and occasionally met with over the years felt likewise.

He had often written to or been in the company of John Masefield, Lady Gregory, Gordon Bottomly, Edmund Blunden, Graham Greene; and through his novelist friend Desmond Chute, Gray made contact with the "Yeats-Ezra Pound-Hauptmann Rappalo group."[2] Various men of letters in turn often mentioned Gray in their letters and books. Hugh Walpole, for one, wrote to Henry James about his reactions to Gray and Raffalovich.[3] Ronald Firbank, for another, placed Gray in his novel *Inclinations* under the name of Father Brown.[4] Geoffrey Grigson, for a third, wrote rather extravagantly of Gray in his *Concise Encyclopedia of Modern World Literature.*[5]

Possibly just reading the works of his literary friends and acquaintances and keeping abreast of modern literature was stimulus enough for Gray to ponder his own creativity. Never a severe critic, he admired most of what his literary friends were writing, and most of them had a measure of admiration for what Gray had written. A few of them suspected that, sooner or later, Gray would write again; and when the pages of *Blackfriars* were available to him, he did not require much persuasion.

Over the next thirteen years, from 1922 to his death in 1934, Gray contributed nineteen poems and sixteen essays to *Blackfriars*, as well as four installments of a novella, *Park*. During this last period of his life, Gray also published a few incidental prose pieces, did a little translating, and composed several devotional works.

Gray's first major work in some thirty years appeared in 1926, a long poem that he entitled *The Long Road*. In the same year, "Sound," the poem that had been excluded from *Silverpoints* some thirty-three years before, was printed. A few years later, in 1932, "Sound" and another poem that had also been excluded from

Silverpoints, "Song of the Stars," were published in John Gawsworth's *Known Signatures*. Several other of Gray's poems were
also being anthologized and being commented upon favorably by
various critics.

Gray would never again merit the attention he had once com-
manded; but just as he had never sought recognition in the nineties,
he did not seek it now. *Silverpoints* had been published in a
limited edition of 250 copies; so, too, was *The Long Road* restricted to 250 copies. Gray's last volume of poetry, *Poems (1931)*,
was published in an even more restricted edition of only 200
copies. And then, in 1932, his last significant publication, *Park: A
Fantastic Story*, was also published in a limited edition of 250
copies.

The Long Road

The Long Road, published in 1926 by Basil Blackwell of Oxford, contains the title poem, as well as "The Flying Fish," four
short incidental poems, and a slightly revised and reordered version
of *Vivis* (a work Gray had published as a pamphlet in 1922)[6]
under the new title of "Quatrains." Bound in cream yellow paper
wrappers, the upper cover of *The Long Road* contains the title
lettered in black within a double rule border. A few copies of a
prepublication issue of the title poem had been privately printed
in a rough draft without its name or the name of the author; these
Gray sent to a few friends for their comments and criticisms.[7]

Basically, *The Long Road* is an allegory of life intermixed with
autobiographical references. In a brief explication for his sister,
Gray noted that "the Road symbolizes life, and its monotony only
is varied with the excursion of the excursionist's own invention ...
The poem contains familiar, strange reflections on the nature of a
road, an artificial river flowing both ways at once."[8]

Gray's reflections on the nature of a road as "an artificial river"
suggests consciousness in its "flowing both ways at once." His extensive use of water imagery further indicates a stream of consciousness.

> The known yet to know;
> a river gliding from and hence
> in utmost calm to thought and sense;
> the effort and its recompense
> at once ebb and flow.

The narrative, with its strong, swinging rhythm, allows the inference that Gray composed parts of the poem while actually on some of his walking tours. Lack of coherence between different sections, and even within some stanzas, can be accounted for through such a manner of composition, albeit the stream of consciousness technique would also allow for certain discontinuities of thought.

The verse form of *The Long Road* is uniquely Gray's. Most of the work is written in five-line stanzas, occasionally prolonged to six or seven lines. In the basic stanza, a shorter line at the beginning rhymes with one as short at the end; and the three longer middle lines make up a triplet. The regularity of rhyme is offset by a flexible meter to create a casual, intimate tone appropriate to the narrative.

Now and then Gray's style, as Ian Fletcher describes it, is "low" and contains a bit of "prattling,"[9] especially in one stanza that visually and onomatopoetically describes migrating geese:

> The goose-gaggle's strength
> defined by cackling overhead
> of broods on Kebnekajse bred
> by one lithe bird a century led
> in great shimmering length.

The pilgrim on the long road that is life is the poet himself. Recollections of his many marathon walks through England and Scotland provide him with matter for reflections upon nature and existence. Etched into his memory are hills he has climbed, dales he has scanned, and streams from which he has drunk. As for the mystery that is life, he now regards his days as being made up of more than one isolated experience followed in time by another.

Accordingly, *The Long Road* plays upon various aspects of time. To emphasize that time can be experienced in a multiplicity of ways, in one particular episode in the poem, "Along Wenlock Edge," Gray utilized the perception of duration as "a march not in space but in time."[10]

The road may be brief or long. One may set out "at noon; / or take the road by rosy light; / or woo the cool and velvet night / ... it all passes soon." Whatever the length of the road, life is

> ...cut off in time,
> Your history is soon compiled;
> a flower observed; a playing child;
> the hemispheric undefiled
>   where white-cloudlets climb.

Traveling along the pathway of life, each pilgrim is bound to encounter certain obstacles. Time demands that he contend with the vicissitudes of existence. Acknowledging that life has its painful experiences, Gray interjects occasional caustic comments:

> The long-aged road
> is tough, resilient and young;
> becomingly abashed among
> the singing streams of earth, so sung;
>   the scored, sacred road.
>
> Its void's counterpart:
> its breath with huddling forms replete,
> and ghosts of those these trudged to meet;
> incessant thunder of their feet
>   and slow beating heart.

Never a wide-eyed optimist, Gray, about the time he penned the above lines, complained to a close friend: "You have not lived if you do not know that there is a pit in life." It may have been fear of the pit, the friend later observed, that "seemed to set Gray apart from those who did not know him, and made him so different from the majority of his fellow-priests."[11]

However negative Gray may have felt at times about life, *The Long Road* is not a deeply pessimistic poem. He was more concerned with depicting various sights, shapes, and sounds, his individual sensate reactions to external nature, than in recording his patrician distaste for the modern world. Any acerbic interludes are subsumed beneath protracted descriptive passages. And despite its length, the regularity of its stanzaic pattern, and a modicum of incoherence, the poem still has a rapidity of motion, an appealing style, readability.

There is much to praise about *The Long Road*, but like everything else Gray wrote, the work has had few readers. As Gray was ever aware, little in the poem would move a large and varied audience. Once again he was content to reach out to only a few select readers; unfortunately, they failed to record their judgments.

Only one brief review of *The Long Road* was published. An unidentified critic had some nice things to say about the poem in *Blackfriars*. Noting that one objection to the work might be that it rambles a bit, he countered that it is exactly what one might expect of something labeled *The Long Road*. The poem, however, he added, is "not disconnected: it does not ramble as a sermon might, or weary you like the rigmarole of empty-headed prattle."[12] Indeed, in his opinion, the work "enthralls, teases, surprises, cheers, exhilarates—in fact, it creates all the moods and emotions that the road arouses."[13] Just as a walk over an old road will reveal fresh joys, he recommended that Gray's poem deserved a second, third, and fourth reading.

Ian Fletcher is the only contemporary critic to have written favorably and perceptively of *The Long Road*. Whatever else the poem may demonstrate, he noted, *The Long Road* makes perfectly clear that "the poet in Gray was broadened, subdued, but not extinguished by the strenuousness of the priest."[14]

"The Flying Fish"

The unidentified critic for *Blackfriars* who wrote so glowingly of *The Long Road* shortly after the poem was published also indicated his admiration for "The Flying Fish." What he especially liked was "the ring and swing and rhythm" of the poem.[15] Other readers, too, were so captivated by the movement, the tempo, the lilt of "The Flying Fish" they did not concern themselves with the narrative or the significance of various lines; but the work, so unlike most of Gray's other poems, implies more than surface meaning.

That Gray himself had a special fondness for "The Flying Fish" can be inferred from its publication history. When first published in 1896 in the fourth issue of the *Dial*, the poem created little interest. It did attract its share of readers, however, and John Masefield was among them. Ten years later, he requested Gray's permission to republish the poem in a collection of nautical verse that he was planning at the time. Gray readily agreed, made a few minor revisions, and "The Flying Fish" appeared in an anthology Masefield entitled *A Sailor's Garland*.[16] "The Flying Fish" now found itself among works of Coleridge, Byron, Tennyson, Browning, Bridges, Kipling, and other well-known British poets who had written of the sea and sailors, of pirates and mermaids.

In 1926, Gray decided to publish "The Flying Fish" once again. This time he would include it in *The Long Road*. Why he decided to republish "The Flying Fish" a third time instead of one of a dozen of other poems he had written is matter for speculation. The most reasonable conjecture is that he had a special fondness for this poem, judged it one of his better efforts, a work that had withstood the test of time. Then, too, "The Flying Fish" probably had some private significance for Gray.

There is nothing to rule out the conjecture that since it was one of the most enigmatic and entertaining things he had written, he would allow his readers to be beguiled and mystified once more. After all, if Yeats, Pound, Eliot, Sitwell, and other contemporaries were publishing esoteric works, vague and allusive poems with all sorts of private and quizzical symbolism, why should he not do the same?

The first impression a reader obtains of "The Flying Fish," however, is that the poem is essentially an ornate tale of an oriental pirate adventuring upon mysterious seas. And yet, the reader slowly begins to realize that "The Flying Fish" is more than rhythmical whimsy, that it is a poem of strange, haunting, imaginative power.

"The Flying Fish" is structured in two parts, both held together by the character of Hang, "the buccaneer / Whom children love and brave men fear," and the one fish that is "fairest of all that be / In the throbbing heart of yonder sea." Thirty-six rhyming quatrains make up Part I, eleven, Part II.

Hang, "master of courage...master of craft," gets the narrative quickly underway:

> Student of wisdom and waterways,
> Course of moons and the birth of days:
> To him in whose heart all things be,
> I bring my story from the sea.

He relates how he "hoists his sail with the broken slats: / Whose lean crew is scarcely food for rats"; that he "creeps from tower top ken" and has "utmost vision of all men." After giving a description of himself, his palace, and his vessel, he focuses upon six strange birds which fly in the farthest sea, "Six...more strange than others be."

> First is the hawk, exceeding great;
> He dwelleth alone, he hath no mate;
> His neck is bound with a yellow ring;
> On his breast is the crest of an ancient king.

> The second bird is exceeding pale,
> From little head to scanty tail;
> She is striped with black on either wing,
> Which is rose-lined like a costly thing.

> Though small the bulk of the brilliant third,
> Of all blue birds 'tis the bluest bird;
> They fly in bands; and seen by day,
> By side of them the sky is grey.

I mind the fifth, I forgot the fourth,
Save that it comes from east by north;
The fifth is an orange white-billed duck;
He diveth for fish like the god of luck.

He hath never a foot on which to stand,
For water yields and he loves not land.
This is the end of many words,
Save one, concerning marvellous birds.

Hang, having dealt with marvellous creatures of the air—"Save
one"—enumerates some fascinating creatures of the sea. He begins
with a great-faced dolphin and a swordfish armed with a hundred
teeth and ends with "The last strange fish...the last strange bird."
This is the Flying Fish, whose enemies are the other five fowl and
the other five fish.

In sea and sky he hath no peace,
For the five strange fish are his enemies.
And the five strange fowl keep watch for him,
They know him well by his crystal gleam.

Often, while Hang has been on his junk's white deck, he has
seen this fish-bird fly through the sky and swoop into the sea.

Scaled bird, how his snout and gills dilate,
All quivering and roseate!
He pants in crystal and mother-of-pearl,
While his body shrinks and his pinions furl.

His beauty passes like bubbles blown;
The white bright bird is a fish of stone.
The bird so fair, for its putrid sake,
Is flung to the dogs in the junk's white wake.

In the second part of the poem, a Sage interprets the Flying Fish
as "a symbol from nature's gear / Of aspirations born of fear."

The Sage remarks that if this Fish could speak, it would say "in his iridescent heart; / I am gorgeous-eyed and a fish apart."

> My heart has secrets of every shell,
> The Hang of fishes knows me well;
> Scales of my breast are softer still,
> The ugly fishes devise my ill.

The Flying Fish prays to "the maker of water-things / Not for a sword, but cricket's wings; / Not to be one of the sons of air." He wants to be rid of water, but he does not wish to be wholly a thing of air.

The Sage offers a final thought on the Flying Fish:

> All his hope is a fear-whipped whim,
> All directions are one to him.
> There are seekers of wisdom no less absurd,
> Son Hang, than the fish that would be a bird.

Taken in its entirety, "The Flying Fish" reads as a distanced image of the aspirations of a poet. The secrets that the work may encapsulate about aspects of Gray's own experiences are not so easily ferreted out. The poem's scenery, its geography, its unusual consonantal collection of words, its ironic, quizzical tone—all initially baffle the reader. Since Gray seldom indulged in obscurity and mystification, but often alluded tangentially to acquaintances and personal affairs in much of his work, the perceptive reader begins to suspect that various fish and fowl in the poem represent specific individuals.

In an essay that Raffalovich wrote for *Blackfriars*, appropriately entitled "Parallels,"[17] he offered some explication. Though what he had to say about "The Flying Fish" is in itself oblique and cryptic, he does provide parallels between various individuals he and Gray knew and the marvellous birds enumerated and described in the poem. For epigraph to his essay, Raffalovich quoted stanzas from "The Flying Fish" relative to the birds, beginning with the hawk and ending with the orange white-billed duck.

The birds do not represent authors, however, but psychics, spiritualists, and clairvoyants whom he and Gray had met at the London Theosophical Society and at seances they attended. Raffalovich and Gray were avid students of the paranormal at the time, and their interests extended all the way from "second sight" and the writing from influx to spiritualism and other parapsychological subjects.

One psychic of interest to Gray and Raffalovich was Ailsa Cassilis. They met sometime in 1895; and it was of her that Raffalovich wrote in "Parallels" that she "sat in Bond Street, semi-Sicilian, semi-Hindoo, and yet blond, a rosy creature with spangles and sequins. For a sovereign she held your hand for a quarter of an hour or so, and prattled prettily about you."[18] This clairvoyant who "cooed" all sorts of "foolish things" to Gray and Raffalovich is described as someone who "could have worn the bluest of plumage," as did the third bird enumerated in "The Flying Fish."[19]

Another psychic that Gray and Raffalovich found interesting was a Miss Yorke, who struck the latter as "a cross between a New Englander and a civil servant's orphan."[20] So gifted was she that, according to her friends, she often helped the police solve their most baffling cases. Her special gift, though, was routing out hidden cards. About her, Raffalovich asks: "Did she come from east by north?" as did the fourth bird.[21]

The fifth bird, who "diveth for fish like the god of Luck," Raffalovich identifies with Cheiro, a medium whose vogue "lasted until he left Paris to be a wine merchant."[22] Not only did he recommend that Raffalovich go in for palmistry, but it was Cheiro who also popularized the prediction that Wilde would die in prison. When Wilde was released from Reading Gaol in 1897, having served his two years at hard labor, and Cheiro was reminded of his unfulfilled prophecy, he coolly replied: "Wait."[23]

Raffalovich concluded his essay by noting that he and Gray were acquainted with far more psychics than Gray alluded to in "The Flying Fish": "All birds are not enclosed in the marvellous aviary of Hang's adventures."[24] They had also known two white peacocks, a peahen, and other birds equally rare, rarae aves that Gray did not hint at in "The Flying Fish" and Raffalovich did not discuss in his "Parallels."

Raffalovich, it would appear, wrote "Parallels" more to explicate one portion of "The Flying Fish" than simply to reminisce about psychics whom he and Gray had known. But why, then, did he not also explicate other equally troublesome portions of the poem? The most reasonable conjecture, perhaps, is that he wrote his essay simply to draw some attention to "The Flying Fish." If that were his chief purpose, he succeeded, for the poem did attract the attention of several critics.

Geoffrey Grigson, in particular, though he never met Gray, became one of his ardent admirers. Gray's poetry, as Grigson reads it, "exemplifies a double problem, of life, and of 'modernism' in literature growing out of the equally queer stuff of 'decadence.' "[25] As for "The Flying Fish," he labeled it Gray's "one finely formed ... unified and entirely successful work of art."[26]

Grigson went on to write favorably about the poem's texture, tone, and movement, and to take the foremost critic of Gray's poetry, Ian Fletcher, to task for not adulating "The Flying Fish." For Fletcher to write about Gray's poetry and not to focus on his "long, hard, sharp, strange single masterpiece," Grigson carped, was to ignore "one of the good 'modern' poems of our century."[27] And for Fletcher not to have singled out "The Flying Fish" as Gray's masterpiece, Grigson further complained quite logically, was tantamount to "assessing Eliot without 'The Waste Land' or Coleridge without 'The Ancient Mariner.' "[28]

Poems (1931)

Gray's gift for metaphor, his use of color and sound, his management of subtle rhythms and effective rhymes are manifest in *Poems (1931)*, the last book of poetry he published. The eighteen poems found in the work are eclectic. Some are biographical; others deal with particular aspects of external nature; a few are essentially religious.

A small booklet of but thirty-seven pages, *Poems (1931)* was designed by Eric Gill and Rene Hague, who also supervised its printing at Pigotts, Buckinghamshire, under the imprint of Sheed and Ward. Measuring 7⅜ by 4¼ inches, the booklet is bound in ivory card wrappers, the upper cover lettered in black with the title and author's name.

Although Gray was not looking for critical acclaim and, indeed, did not bother to send out copies of the work for review, *Poems (1931)* did attract some attention. Being quite different from his previous verse publication, this work impressed those who read it. The themes and technique were uniquely his, but what he had written resembled what was being written by the more modern exponents of poetic expression. Several critics commented that Gray had found a new voice, a more distinctive style.

Gray, obviously, had read the poetry of the Georgians, several of whom he knew personally. Then, too, he was drawn to the later poetry of Yeats, whom he had known at the Rhymers' Club. Finally, he was also reading the works of Ezra Pound, T. S. Eliot, Edith Sitwell, and other leading figures.[29] Contemporary poets were having an influence upon Gray, just as he, directly and indirectly, had had an influence upon them. They knew, of course, of his early translations of Baudelaire, Verlaine, Mallarmé, and Rimbaud, and the creative role he played in introducing French Symbolism into English literature. Unfortunately most of Gray's contemporaries in the twenties did not comment specifically upon his later work, nor did he comment upon theirs.

The prominent Georgian poet Edmund Blunden is an exception, however, for he commented favorably on *Poems (1931)*. "I shall not see truer and more imaginative poetry in my time," he wrote.[30] One poem he especially liked is entitled "Ode," a work that Blunden held would always serve as an excellent example of Gray's ability to express hidden, indefinable qualities.

On one level, "Ode" is a glorification of external nature; on another, it details a surging of creative thought. The opening lines in particular imply poetic inspiration, an opening of the floodgates of the imagination.

Open, opal doors,
mists that roaming strew
long unvisited moors;
open, womb of the rain, lap of the dew;
let run its winding course
through
peat and moss
the slender hidden force;
and the bird sing, sing,
even to a note unheard in the unflected blue,
to a still listening ear,
where hillocks roll and grasses toss
in the light wistful year.

Playing upon the "well-springs" of creativity and a "new-born rillet" actually observed in nature, Gray follows the course of both through their tortuous ways,

While windmills still gesticulate,
dip, motionless, the river seems to wait
upon the first salt kisses of the ocean's lips;
where the white pharos heeds the ships.

The lines that follow, rich in imagery, continue to paint pictures of water in motion, of a stream rushing along on its journey to the sea. One moment it swerves "to shun a miniature rock." Later, "when the waters narrow and rise, / with an action of fetched breath," the pulsating stream rounds and plunges "as to the hazard of death." Then it takes repose "into a well-like, deep, tree-shaded pool; / where a school / of light and dark flecks play and hide."

During the nineties, Gray had been more concerned with virtuosity than originality. For him to be a poet then consisted mainly in digesting, assimilating, translating. As a "modern" poet, like so many of his contemporaries, what he wrote now took its origin from the data of his own life, his personal observations, his individualized thoughts.

"Audi Alteram Partem" is a case in point. Although this poem may at first seem intentionally personal, allusive, cryptic, those close to Gray were cognizant of its full meaning. The opening stanza reads:

> France you remember, Dominic,
> adjusted an accursed thing
> until it made a dead man sing.
> A queer, unnecessary trick.

The key that unlocks this quatrain's meaning lies in the identification of *France* and *Dominic* and the former's fondness for recordings of Italian opera. The *France* of the first line was Reverend Samuel France, D.D., who like Gray had once been a student at The Scots College, Rome. From 1917 to 1924, he was in charge of St. Mary's, Haddington; but more important to an understanding of "Audi Alteram Partem" is the fact that he was passionately fond of music. The *Dominic* addressed was the Reverend Dominic Hart, a priest of the diocese of St. Andrews and Edinburgh, who also had studied at The Scots College.

The poem continues:

> Caruso marred the cosy night
> until we bravely sued for peace
> to stretch our limbs again at ease
> and listen to the storm outside.

One night when Gray and Hart were guests of France at Haddington, France insisted upon playing a recording of Verdi's *Aida* over and over again to a sickening extreme. Though not indifferent to Caruso's great voice, Gray grew tired of the tenor's arias and sought an excuse for bed.

The experience, not one that Gray would have wanted to recollect in tranquillity, could not be readily forgotten. He may even have written "Audi Alteram Partem" in an attempt to free his memory of the event.[31] As for the Latin title of the poem, it recommends that the reader should "listen to another part"—that is, Gray's reactions to a less than satisfying evening. And yet, the delightful wit and playful insinuations of the remaining six stanzas suggest that there was really no ill will on his part.

"Audi Alteram Partem" is the most personal and allusive of all Gray's 1931 poems, but to a large extent everything that he was writing during this period of his life was particular to his own experiences. Even his nature poetry came directly from his minute observations of plants, flowers, and shrubs. During his many walking tours of England, the Highlands, Banffshire and Aberdeenshire, of France and Iceland, he spent countless hours in a study of various aspects of nature.

On one of his long walks, for instance, he became fascinated with the anemone. He had of course read Shakespeare's "Venus and Adonis" and knew well the story about the flower springing from the blood of Adonis, the beloved of Venus, after he had been gored to death by a wild boar; but in his poem "Anemone," Gray rejected myth to focus upon nature in the concrete. With a kind of scientific curiosity he examined this windflower of the crowfoot family and wrote of it personally as:

> The flower I once in fancy praised
> is yet my peerless friend,
> in loveliness aware, effaced,
> until its glories end.

Intrigued by the anemone's white, purple, and red cut-shaped flowers which seemed to dilate under the influence of a gentle breeze, and to depict its unique, delicate beauty, he wrote:

> Three colors in the petals swim
> and freely interchange,
> or leaping bright, or sunk or dim,
> a long chromatic range.

The beauty, the delicacy of the anemone appealed to Gray no less than the loftiness, the strength of closely planted privets that served as boundaries, barriers, fences. Just as Robert Burns sang in a most rustic strain of his Scottish fields, so Gray could not restrain his more sophisticated poetic reaction to the ubiquitous hedgerows that interlaced the countryside. In "The English Hedge" he wrote:

> Cornell of bitter fruit and ruddy hues;
> music of its hidden zithers these;
> coral, and even ruby, manganese
> which cheere-cheeks and apple-skins suffuse.

> Strides of bramble in its summer march
> along the wall of leaves and down the bank
> pushes its tender trust and pearly fangs
> dust, drought and weariness at length shall parch.

In the next four stanzas, Gray delineates the "lissom vines" of the hedge, its "enchanted foam" of white blossoms, its "mighty weavings of...limbs," and concludes with

> the brute
> determination of its supple strength
> and sinewy purpose not to be displaced.
> Leaves gay shields at a joust, green, gold and black;
> or in armoury hung, so duly spaced.

The sensuousness of Gray's diction, his appeal to the eye and ear, in the above lines harkens back to his nineties' verse; yet its vibrancy indicates actuality, not artificiality. At one time, Gray would have agreed with Wilde that art was superior to nature, that a poet might just as well sit with his back to the countryside, but "The English Hedge" is an obvious glorification of the natural over the artificial. Now, in his love for nature, Gray could rhapsodize over a majestic mountain, a sparkling stream, a shrub, a flower. Those responsive to their Creator, Gray apparently wished to demonstrate in his nature poems of 1931, easily recognize Him in His handiwork.

As though to stress that there was nothing pantheistic about his nature poetry, Gray concluded *Poems (1931)* with three specifically religious works. The first two, "Mane Nobiscum Domine" and "Speciosae et Delicatae Assimilavi Filiam Sion," owe their origin to Gray's familiarity with and high regard for the Roman liturgy; the last, "The Lord Looks at Peter," is more personal in tone and springs mainly from a troublesome period in Gray's life.

"Mane Nobiscum Domine" is a well-crafted poem in which the Disciples at Pentecost plead with Christ to remain with them.

> Stay with us, Lord, the day is travelled fast;
> we meet thee at its close.
> Lord, at our humble table sit and share,
> and be, our sweet repose.

Two more stanzas echo the Disciples' love for and trust in Christ. The final stanza reads:

> We cannot be without thee, Lord, because
> the night is perilous;
> and anxiously our earthly journey draws
> to evening; stay with us.

"Speciosae et Delicatae Assimilavi Filiam Sion," despite its cumbersome title, is another simple, direct poem of love and trust. Both in its rhythm and manner of interrogation, it bears a close resemblance to an Easter sequence, the "Laud Sion," which is addressed to Mary Magdalene and seeks to elicit from her news of the Risen Christ; but the subject of Gray's poem is the first Christmas.

In the opening stanzas, the first two lines contain words from an interlocutor, the concluding two, the responses of the shepherds in the manger.

> Tell us, shepherds, what you saw;
> tell us, were you not afraid?
> We saw the king in glory laid,
> a babe, upon a little straw.

> Neither of you was afraid;
> neither were you filled with awe?
> We saw him lying on the straw,
> the baby; and we saw the maid.

In the concluding stanza, the wisdom lacking in sophisticates is found in the direct answer of the simple shepherds:

> Shepherds twain, who speak so fair,
> lead the way to Bethlehem.
> An angel guide us to them;
> And Bethlehem is everywhere.

Of greater interest than "Speciosae et Delicatae Assimilavi Filiam Sion" or "Mane Nobiscum Domine," perhaps, is "The Lord Looks at Peter." On a primary level, this poem is a consequence of Gray's devotion to the Prince of Apostles. His special interest in St. Peter is apparent in the naming of that majestic edifice in Edinburgh built in 1906 through the lavish generosity of André Raffalovich—of which Gray was rector for some twenty-seven years—St. Peter's Church.[32]

· Gray dedicated his church to St. Peter partly after his Roman memories, but the main reason he did so was that he too, like Peter, had had his unregenerate days. At his initial conversion in 1890, Gray had a measure of the overconfidence characteristic of the Apostle who later denied Christ. Like another Peter, Gray did likewise. Peter later came to abhor his denial, as did Gray when he underwent his second conversion in 1894. Gray's four-year repudiation of Christ, as one of his clerical friends expressed it, "was for him always a matter of infinite regret."[33]

"The Lord Looks at Peter," accordingly, questions the sincerity of a love that failed under trial. Peter is the speaker, but the voice of Gray can be heard whispering of the diffidence that had welled up within him:

> My lips were like my steps a song,
> and all my thoughts of Follow Me;

but when the march was overlong
I turned away from thee.

When not alone thine eyes, my God,
but all thy sacred body wept,
and every tear was ruby blood,
I shut my eyes and slept.

A night alarm; a weaponed crowd;
one blow, and with the rest I ran;
I warmed my hands, and said aloud:
I never knew the man.

Chapter Six

A Novella and Some Essays

Park: A Fantastic Story

Toward the end of 1930, Gray began work on a novella, *Park: A Fantastic Story*. Unlike *The Person in Question*, his other important work of fiction—which he had written some forty years before but never published—*Park* was a work that Gray was determined to see in print. When it was brought to the attention of the editors of *Blackfriars*, they expressed interest in the work. Ordinarily, *Blackfriars* did not publish fiction, but agreement was reached to publish excerpts from *Park*.

The first selection appeared in the November 1931 issue, a second in January 1932, followed by a third in March and a fourth in April.[1] Appended to the fourth excerpt were the words "To be continued"; but there was no sequel. Gray had already decided to publish *Park* in its entirety.

Eric Gill and Rene Hague had been approached to design the book. Out of a high regard for Canon Gray, the literary merits of *Park* as they perceived them, and their own aesthetic standards, they wanted to create a volume that would be exquisite yet unpretentious. For the cover, a rose-red cloth back and gray paperboards seemed most appropriate. The text, they felt, demanded the choicest handmade paper. They commissioned Denis Tegetmeier to do a copperplate etching; he decided on a frontispiece depicting the two groups of men that Gray focused on in his novel. Finally, in April 1932, Sheed and Ward published the book.

122

Park fulfilled the hopes of its author, its designers, and its illustrator. Each had done all that he could to satisfy his own fastidious taste, but there still remained the taste of the public. Though the book was not meant for the crass reader, there was concern over how even its select readers and perceptive critics might respond. To appreciate, one must understand, but to what extent would those few readers drawn to *Park* understand and appreciate?

The title of Gray's novella provided no difficulty, coming as it does from the name of its protagonist, Dr. Mungo Park, a priest and seminary professor of moral theology. In many ways, however, Reverend Park is Reverend Gray himself, and much that Gray recounts under the guise of fiction is autobiography. Not only are both in their early sixties, but Park's character embodies several of Gray's own attributes. Physically, they are the same man, athletic and well proportioned, balding slightly, and even missing four teeth.[2] More important, the eponymous hero of the work is spiritually and psychologically akin to Gray himself.

Like his fictional counterpart, Gray loved to go on long walking tours, and one of his favorite spots was the Cotswolds, the locale of the novella. One day, when out walking along the Oxford road near Burford, Park undergoes a paranormal experience. He has a sudden illusion of death. When did it happen and how, he wonders. Bringing his emotions under control, he hypothesizes about life and death. He concludes that he cannot be dead, that somehow his sentient being has been transported into the remote future. His stick still hangs on his wrist, and he can hear his watch ticking. He verifies that his many pockets still hold his map, handkerchief, pencil, knife, keys, and rosary.

Park comes to realize that somehow he is now in another dimension of time. The place is still the Cotswold Hills of southwestern England, but the populace has changed. A highly cultivated race of blacks, the Wampani, have taken over the country. The original Anglo-Saxon inhabitants are now living a troglodytic existence beneath the surface of the earth.

The progeny of the former inhabitants of the Cotswolds are in-

frahuman creatures, animalistic in their ways, socially and spiritually retarded. They live in a maze of winding, branching tunnels,
in vast caverns. During some remote period the caverns had been
excavated and strengthened with consummate engineering skill.

Fascinated by his first meeting with one of these underground
men, Park laments that the specimen he closely observes is like
"a rodent in whom age had emphasized the features of the race,
adding all the insults time matures; who wore, most horribly,
great convex amber spectacles."[3] After observing more of these
underground men, Park is forced to conclude that this subterranean
population is "a dreadful type...with no variety that he could
distinguish."[4] Their eyes, large and prominent, are always looking
to right and left, rabbit style. Their noses are hooked, their teeth,
prominent. Rodents all, he thinks.

Their microcosm suggests a world that has anticipated or experienced a holocaust. If a totally destructive war has taken place,
the surface of the earth has somehow recovered; but the descendants
of the original underground inhabitants still keep to their elaborate
fall-out shelters. Park learns that in the dim and distant past they
had gone underground never to emerge. Even they do not know
why their ancestors tunneled under the earth.

The Wampani, on the other hand, prefer light and air, the
open spaces of the countryside. They are humane, religious, tech-
nologically advanced. They dwell in houses that are long, low, vast,
with broad eaves, balconies, and circular windows. Aristocratic and
highly educated, the Wampani communicate with Park in the
sacred language, as they call Latin, since they cannot speak his
tongue nor he theirs.

Though he is as much an enigma to them as they are to him, the
Wampani treat Park well. When Park learns they are Roman
Catholics and live in a theocratic state, he reveals that he is a
priest. They inquire the name of his bishop and the date of his
ordination. Unable to verify either, the Wampani are suspicious of
Park's claim, and he is denied his priestly office. Since he cannot
give a satisfactory accounting of himself, and the Wampani can-

not fathom how "the pale man" has come among them, his official status is that of one "legally dead."

Technically, Park is a prisoner. He is not denied freedom of movement, but he has certain civil disabilities. Even more, he is baffled by a Kafkaesque sense of restriction, of repression, of timelessness. And now, with considerable narrative skill, Gray allows the reader to experience Park's perceptions as he passes slowly from one bewilderment to another.

To begin with, instead of addressing Park by his name, the Wampani refer to him as Drak. Has he been given a new name? Is *Park* simply being confused or mispronounced? Is his name being transliterated into their language? Why is he once—and only once—addressed as Dom Monaco Parek? What significance his new appellations may have Park cannot fathom.

A friendship he is able to establish with another "legally dead" man he hopes will provide him with some answers to his predicament. The "legally dead" man is Dlar, who had formerly been known as Dom Egid Reni. Dlar, Park learns, had once been condemned to death, but then was granted amnesty; nevertheless, Dlar cannot exercise a profession, bring an action, or be a witness, have servants, hunt, or publish books. Dlar conceals what his offense has been, but this becomes unimportant when Park discovers that Dlar is a keen student of the vanished English civilization.

In time, the Wampani come to accept the fact that, like many of themselves, Park is an ordained priest. The Wampani take their religion seriously; indeed, Catholicism permeates all aspects of their lives. Little wonder, then, that Park is eventually welcomed among them. After he is duly enfranchised and ennobled, he is initiated into aspects of their language and customs.

The Wampani speak Bapama, a language with an involved grammar and extensive vocabulary. Being something of a linguist, Park masters this non-Indo-European language from a Bapama-English lexicon and grammar. One Bapama expression that Park finds especially interesting is the proverb *Pash Zezel Tiffem*, which he learns means "the darkest wine illuminates."

The Wampani method of enumeration is unusual and causes Park some difficulty. He tries to explain to them, for example, that in decimal enumeration, he is sixty years old. According to his calculation, he states, he had been born 114 years before; yet the Wampani, who have a complete list of every birth in its proper genealogical setting for the last thousand years, insist that he must be thousands of years old.

After spending an indefinite amount of time among the Wampani, at the end of the story Park again—as he did at the beginning—fears that he may be dying. "He moved along the top edge of the valley, gently rocked in his spirit by the circumstances: the light and loneliness; when it struck him that something was going a bit too far. He thought he would sit down, or perhaps lie down. He had sometimes foolish apprehensions about his heart. He heard a long musical note, which made him think he was ill. He had an illusion of false memory.... He or another said: I am afraid he is dead."[5]

When at last he opens his eyes, he is back in the world of reality: "It was the most lovely of spring days; and he walked on slowly, recovering his soul. What a world! The hedges were still white with fruit trees in flower and the ground was wild with celandine, wood anemone, violets, some primroses.... It affected him as the natural scene did under that sort of restorative fatigue."[6] Just as he had walked into a dream world, he now walked out of it. And so Park continues his walk and arrives in Malmesbury in time for tea.

Perplexed about his paranormal experience, his reverie, Park consults his physician. Likewise perplexed by what he hears but wishing to put Park at rest, the physician explains: "You were asleep...; it was not a faint. It was a short, deep sleep; and what you experienced was a waking state."[7] As difficult as it is for Park to believe that he has been in a short sleep and has had a long dream, he cannot refute his physician. To reassure Park, the physician adds that though the period of slumber was brief, Park's dream was simply—in the last words of the novel—"somewhat more elaborate than usual."[8]

The Genesis of *Park*

Different works that Gray had read contributed in their own way to *Park*. He had of course read a great deal of travel and utopian literature, as well as a great deal of fantastic fiction. His reading of such futuristic works as Morris's *News from Nowhere*, Wells's *The Time Machine*, and E. M. Forster's "The Machine Stops" probably made the strongest impression upon his imagination.

Like *News from Nowhere*, *Park* depicts a feudal society showing the kind of pastoral utopian existence that Morris so favored. *The Time Machine* looks far into a future in which all humanity is divided into two groups, as it is in *Park*, though Wells's concentration upon stunted, brutish creatures who live underground and feed upon aesthetic, childlike individuals must have been repellent to Gray. Like *The Time Machine*, "The Machine Stops" is yet another story set in a future period in which all life has withdrawn below the surface of the earth; from this work of Forster's, Gray could have borrowed the "strange speaking room" in which Park finds himself, a room with apparatus foreshadowing the wonders of television.

Mungo Park's *Travels in the Interior of Africa* (1799) also influenced Gray. The name of the Scottish explorer suggested to Gray the name he would give the protagonist of his novella; yet when the fictional Park is asked the origin of his curious appellation by the Wampani, he responds facetiously that *Mungo* is the name of a little-known saint and that *Park* in his language signifies an enclosed recreational property. Of greater importance is the fact that Gray knew the explorer had encountered blacks in Africa. Blacks were simple savages to the original Mungo Park, but the fictional Park discovers that the blacks in the England of the future are eminently civilized men.

There are several reasons why Gray reversed the customary racial stereotype. One can be found in a statement made by his sister, Sister Mary Raphael. She recalled that when her brother was a young man, he was deeply interested in the black man, that he used to say that "although he was a white man he was black inside,"[9] and that he foretold in a general way that some day the black man would rule. When Gray first developed such admiration for the black race that he preferred to think of himself as a black man at heart, Sister Mary Raphael unfortunately failed to specify; but it is noteworthy that in his novella, Gray has one character say to Park: "Drak, your skin is white, more's the pity; but you are black inside."[10]

An additional reason for Gray's interest in blacks is that his younger brother Alexander, who served in the British army, married a black woman, and their son was later educated by Dominicans in England. Finally, when Gray was at The Scots College he encountered black seminarians who were in Rome preparing for the priesthood. The occasional black among so many white students prompted Gray to reflect upon the future of the church in Africa and what kind of Catholics blacks might ultimately become.

Style and Meaning

Befitting its subject matter, *Park* has a quality of the poetic and the timeless. There are few lengthy descriptive passages in the work, other than those that dwell on the Cotswold landscape. Gray paints the Cotswolds in the diction and imagery of the poet, focusing on "earth and sky; the familiar golden soil and cool green, the coloured patterns of fields, crop, stubble, grazing, early plowing; hedges of quick, draped with clematis and tangled with black bryony. The eastern sky was a dense formation of thin, horizontal clouds."[11]

Having the Cotswold earth and sky for backdrop gives the story an element of reality. Gray also carefully worked out such factors as language, costumes, diet, architecture, interior design, and even a televisionlike "speaking room" in order to bestow touches of reality upon the narrative. The dialogue, however, often creates a different impression.

Descriptions of the Cotswolds and casual references to the plausibility of the Wampani are handled in a mannered, deliberately understated fashion that slows down the pace. The dialogue, on the other hand, speeds up the story. The result: a counterpointing of visual and aural effects. Then, to connote the timelessness he sought, Gray omitted quotation marks from the many conversations in which Park so frequently engages. One day, for example, there is an exchange between Park and one of the Wampani on the thorny question of Park's origin and age.

You say you are 60, he said, with a charming malicious smile, which obliterated the last vestige of his anger. We do not believe any of your statements of the kind.

> You do not believe me? But here I am; I am in physical
> and mental health. I give an account of myself with
> its myriad particulars, which are all harmonious.

I believe you in a desperate, syllogistic way.... But that you were born 114 years ago, I must deny; for we have proof that you are older. That you were born in Ia, on the same wild and contradictory understanding, I absolutely deny; for we have a complete list of every birth, in its proper genealogical setting... for the last thousand years.[12]

Other conversational passages scattered throughout the novella are just as terse; some are dreamlike. The oneiric nature of much of the dialogue almost makes it seem that Gray is at times simply recounting puzzling episodes from his more unusual dreams; but, then, as has so often been said, the artist dreams while he is awake. *Park* is a sustained effort of Gray's imagination, the result of his creative mind, a work of art but a piece of fantasy as well. And once *Park* is categorized as a fantasy, it is tempting to search for some hidden meaning in Park's dream, some involved allegory behind Gray's surface narrative.

Like any work of art worth thinking about seriously, *Park* might be interpreted in a number of ways. Was he, for example, pondering the high-low dualism of human life in his depiction of the two groups of individuals Park encounters? Bernard Bergonzi, who has made a special study of *Park*, does not believe it fruitful to delve into any of the philosophical complexities the novella presents.

That the work may have symbolical overtones, he readily admits. But in his opinion, the chief effects of *Park* are to be found on the surface. As Bergonzi reads *Park*, it is essentially a dramatization of "the problem of the loss of identity...but without deep mythic power."[13]

Alexandra Zaina, another Gray specialist, is also of the opinion that despite symbolic overtones *Park* does not have any special esoteric dimensions; yet she admits to being troubled by a feeling that the story may have unsuspected levels of meaning. She questions, for example, the purpose of a map made up of straight lines, ragged forms, and unknown signs which a Monsignor Villa Gracil shows Park, forcing him—and the reader—to piece together anew the geography of England.[14] She also wonders if there might be a code which would make the names of Drak, Dlar, and such other characters as Svillig, Ini'in, Villa Gracil more intelligible.

An onomastic study of the names of various characters, regrettably, does not indicate any discernible pattern. Proceeding from the known to the unknown reveals nothing. That Drak is Park, Gray informs the reader. Another character, A Ra, who dedicates an oratory to St. Sebastian, is clearly André Raffalovich. Other names, however, are not so obvious; indeed, they are impossible to decipher. They could represent various individuals Gray knew, but, lacking clues, the reader remains baffled. If there is some special meaning to place names, or the blacks being labeled Wampani and their language being designated Bapama, Gray does not even hint an explanation.

After speculating upon such questions and not arriving at satisfactory answers, critics are forced to conclude that we may never fathom completely all that is implicit in *Park*. The novella remains something of a verbal curiosity. There is no key that will open the narrative to a particular meaning. If there were, Gray has failed to give reasonable hints. At best, he parceled out what he may have intended into disparate elements. There is no disagreeing with Brocard Sewell's contention that *Park* cannot be categorized or classified: "it is part science-fiction, part novel of ideas."[15]

Despite its troublesome ambiguities, *Park* has drawn its share of critics. A critic for the *Times Literary Supplement* was not especially satisfied with the novella. Reading with a captious eye, he dismissed the work as "the kind of thing art for art's sake comes to in the long run."[16] That the novella might appeal to some readers depended upon whether one took to Gray's style: "a blend of Firbankian preciosity with a sort of avuncular sacerdotal jollity."[17] *Park* had certain qualities, he conceded; but it was on the whole "undisciplined and self-indulgent."[18] A critic for the *Manchester Guardian* preferred to discuss *Park* as science fiction. Now and then, he pointed out, the novella even attained to the superior qualities found in Kafka and Firbank.[19]

John Pope-Hennessy, who reviewed *Park* for *Blackfriars*, was more enthusiastic. *Park*, he proposed, has "a distinctive quality" which makes it "a remarkable and sometimes beautiful book."[20] Among several critics who agree with Pope-Hennessy is Brocard Sewell. "*Park* is a small masterpiece," he contends. "Its prose is pure."[21] Alexandra Zaina also rates *Park* the most important of Gray's prose writings: "a minor masterpiece."[22] *Park* is proof enough for her that Gray was "far more than a fossilized survival of an earlier day."[23]

Bernard Bergonzi goes even further. Willing to concede that *Park* reveals some of its author's weaknesses, Bergonzi feels that the novella is nonetheless Gray's most sustained imaginative achievement. He recommends that this "curiously timeless work... deserves a niche in the history of modern English fiction."[24] Bergonzi especially admires the novella for its "mannered and deliberately understated mode of narration... which recalls the laconic precision of the best of Gray's verse."[25]

Park, nevertheless, has never been—nor will it likely ever be—a popular book. Its subjectivity of treatment so limits appeal that only two editions of the novella have ever been published.[26] At the moment there is little demand for a third printing. Popularity is relative at best, and Gray never sought mass appeal; still, he may have wished that this unusual piece of fiction had the quality to attract a larger share of readers than it has.

Fully aware of the rather restrictive nature of *Park*, one critic was moved to remark that the work "has the dryness of a patrician wine."[27] His apt metaphor is perhaps the best critical summation of *Park*—its brilliant style, its overall quality, its limited appeal.

Blackfriars Essays

During the last period of his life, from 1922 to 1934, Gray was a steady contributor of essays to *Blackfriars*. Most of these essays treat of nature; some are reflective, interpretive, analytical; a few are mainly descriptive.

Though none of the essays has ever been reprinted, Alexandra Zaina maintains they deserve to figure prominently in any anthology of the period. An obvious devotee of Gray's prose, she notes that even in the nineties, Gray had eschewed the highly wrought vocabulary and hothouse imagery that characterized so much of the prose writing of his contemporaries, that Gray exercised moderation and invariably utilized a precise choice of words and skillful understatement. "These are the qualities that remain and are perfected in his latter years," she points out, "spiced by a curious dry humor and an ever-fantastic imagination."[28]

The first of Gray's *Blackfriars* essays, "God-Made and Machine-Made," appeared late in 1924.[29] As its title indicates, this essay is a general discussion of the machine, its benefits and limitations. That Gray would compose such an essay may at first seem strange, until it is recalled that artists and theologians have written almost as much about machines as have economists and social reformers.

Gray obviously was familiar with the reactions to the machine expressed by Carlyle, Dickens, Ruskin, Morris, and other prominent Victorian figures. He was well aware that most Victorians never really came to terms with the aesthetic implications of technology, that their writings on the machine betrayed their inability to distinguish between the moral and artistic aspects of industrialization.[30] Not wishing to concern himself with the social or economic ramifications of technology and industrialization, Gray quickly concedes that machines have done much for mankind. He does not argue against their place in modern life; rather, he focuses primarily on the need for good design.

Writing more from the vantage point of artist and poet than priest and theologian, Gray maintains that even machines themselves have to be well designed, as well as the objects they turn out. And after suggesting two or three more aspects of design and manufacturing, he concludes his essay by stressing that human intelligence must direct the machine and supply what it lacks. His last sentence is aphoristic: "Machine and servant should be servile, and man its master magisterial."[31]

While Gray states his own individualized views in "God-Made and Machine-Made," an essay he wrote the following year, 1925, is even more personal in tone. In "Winter Walking,"[32] he expatiates freely on this vigorous form of exercise he himself so frequently enjoyed. After listing some of the basic equipment needed—good boots worn over two pairs of socks, a Bartholomew half-inch map, and "a good conscience"—he goes on to examine the essence of walking, which he pursues as an image of life: "It is leaving that which is present and returning by a safe journey to that which was never distant; an ambit in imaginery space, where sensation is fruitful, its fruits imperishable."[33] The motion of walking, Gray posits, accords with cosmic rhythms.

As a Decadent poet of the nineties, Gray tended to disdain nature as inferior to art, but during his long tramps about England, Scotland, and Iceland, he came to admire the extraordinary beauty he perceived in landscapes and skies. In an essay he wrote in 1926, "Excursions,"[34] he describes a particular walk over the Tweed to Yarrowdale and St. Mary's Loch that he enjoyed that year.

"An Island Cloud-Factory"[35] is a sequel of sorts to "Excursions," for in this essay Gray continues with his adulation of nature. The locale this time is the Isle of Skye. This largest of the Inner Hebrides strikes him as a place that exists mainly to manufacture clouds: "High white round-headed pillar-like 'Sunday clouds' for little Presbyterians; fuel for the blazing sunsets of the arctic; clouds for all purposes, general, scientific, aesthetic and domestic;

clouds to keep the sky dry and the earth moist; all kinds of clouds."[36]

"The Parting Guest"[37] is another essay of serenity and comfort; but, as its title indicates, it dilates upon both the hospitality of the countryside and the necessity of returning, sooner or later, to urban life. Ever the poet, even when his medium was prose, Gray writes: "As the hospitality of a region is almost elemental, parting from it must be a distributed anguish if it is to be borne, for stones and rushing water are hosts, lines of horizon engrave their delicacy upon the contemplative soul, chill and damp corrode, drenching rain and hip-deep snow are not so easily forgotten."[38] Such a sentence is a good example of the poetic diction and rhythmical prose found in all of Gray's *Blackfriars* essays.

Throughout most of these essays, Gray makes constant allusions to art and literature. A memorable example appears in "Cyder."[39] After an abrupt beginning—"Cider is vile stuff"—he proceeds to examine its usual ingredients, apples, turnips and water, and then writes: "They [apples] may be teased out of a tree...by pre-Raphaelite girls, illogically mounted on ladders leaned against a mass of leaves and twigs; and fall into the paddock where the nephews may be nude, and blobs of sunlight lie on them and on baskets."[40] The ambiguity of such an allusion required Gray to add that Charles Shannon depicted such scenes in his lithographs.

Several more of Gray's essays treat of external nature just as admirably, but the last essay he wrote for *Blackfriars*—indeed the very last thing he wrote, aside from some incidental letters—focuses on human nature, the character, disposition, tendencies of the one person whom he knew better than any other. "André Raffalovich"[41] is a brief discourse on the life and passing of his friend and companion of some forty years.

On the morning of February 14, 1934, when a carriage arrived to take Raffalovich to mass at St. Peter's Church, as it had arrived for almost thirty years, it was discovered that he had died in his sleep. Canon Gray was sent for immediately. Raffalovich had reached his seventy-fourth year, had grown rather frail, but his death had not seemed imminent.

Raffalovich's passing was duly noted in the press, but Gray felt that something additional should be said, that he should offer a personal tribute to his departed friend. Never one to express himself effusively or at great length, Gray, in writing his final piece for *Blackfriars*, limited himself to fourteen short paragraphs, in all, fewer than 750 words.

In his testimonial, Gray did not allude to himself or mention his long association with Raffalovich. Instead, he concentrated upon Raffalovich's thirty years in Edinburgh, noting that for his departed friend, social life had been something of an art. He also called attention to Raffalovich's natural gifts, "the base of which was a properly pivoted intelligence...elastic memory...facility with languages; the disquieting alertness of his mind."[42]

Alongside Raffalovich's natural gifts, Gray emphasized, grew and flourished an abundant kindness which found expression among a multitude of friends. But for him to write at great length of such matters now, Gray commented, would border on betrayal. The highest praise that Gray allowed himself to bestow upon his recently deceased friend was to end his mild encomium with a reference to Raffalovich's ever-charitable disposition.

About the same time that his brief eulogy of Raffalovich appeared in print, Gray was taken seriously ill. He was found to be suffering from congestion of the lungs and pleurisy. A few weeks later, on June 14, 1934, exactly four months to the day after the death of his lifelong companion, Canon John Gray joined André Raffalovich in death.

Chapter Seven

Conclusion

Almost fifty years have elapsed since the death of John Gray, but his reputation has not faded. Indeed, bibliographical evidence indicates that his works are slowly becoming more widely known. This is not to say that he is widely recognized among devotees of English literature. At best, he has had an appeal only to a limited number of readers.

Aside from a few troublesome details, most of the important aspects of Gray's life are known; nonetheless, even those familiar with such facts and his literary accomplishments regard him as a somewhat elusive figure. How important a writer he was in the nineties even his friends and contemporaries could not quite decide. Though he was often invited to read his poetry at the Rhymers' Club, he was never an official member, nor was his work published in either of their anthologies.

Lionel Johnson dismissed him as "a sometimes beautiful oddity."[1] Ernest Dowson, on the other hand, admired Gray and often addressed him as *Poeta Optime*.[2] As Johnson and Dowson both knew, there was some truth to the charge that at first Gray was more interested in playing the role of a man of letters than in actually being one; yet when he decided to play the role in earnest, he won the admiration of Wilde, Pater, Beardsley, and a host of other well-known nineties' figures.

Frank Harris, for one, commented that Gray had "great personal distinction" and "charming manners"; and though Harris had a greater all-round admiration for Wilde than he did for

Gray, he still believed that Gray had "a marked poetic gift, a much greater gift than Oscar possessed."[3] Another of Wilde's friends, Ada Leverson, hailed Gray as "the incomparable poet of the age."[4] Harris and Leverson felt that Gray was worthy of such adulation because in his poetry, as they read it, he was doing more than simply being derivative, delicate, and clever.

To a considerable extent, Gray had been influenced by Wilde, and it was usual to assume that any parallels in their works were a consequence of the younger, less famous writer borrowing from his older, more successful mentor. Gray could do little to disabuse those who liked to so theorize, for seldom was the subject of "borrowing" mentioned in front of him. One day, however, a few years after Wilde's death, when he was out enjoying an early spring walk with a fellow priest, Gray remarked on the fairy-like greenery of the trees, the buds showing their faint tips, on their "shrill" green.

"I have just met that epithet in Wilde's *De Profundis*," the priest friend somewhat impertinently remarked. For several seconds, Gray remained quiet; then he responded with suppressed annoyance: "When we met in the terrible cenacle of poets [the Rhymers' Club], we used to recite our poems to one another. I remember having composed a sonnet on spring and reciting duly; and ... I remember that Oscar Wilde was one of the company. Would you like to hear it?"

Abashed beyond measure, Gray's priest friend murmured, "Please." Without a falter, Gray recited the sonnet, which included the epithet "shrill." He made his point. "So you see," he concluded, "Wilde may have been the plagiarist."[5]

Gray was prompted to respond as strongly as he did for he was always being compared with Wilde, or Dowson, or Johnson, or Yeats, or some other nineties' figure who had achieved greater fame than he. And yet, Gray never really sought the limelight. If it did shine upon him momentarily, he invariably retreated from its rays.

There are so many contradictions about Gray, the man, the priest, that any attempt to sum up his life is fraught with the danger of oversimplification. To evaluate him as a poet, fiction writer, and essayist is no less difficult. Practically every book written about the nineties mentions his name, but allusions to him or his work are often so casual that he would seem to be at best an insignificant figure. The same critics who too quickly consign him to a literary limbo are usually those least familiar with his poetry. To know his poetry is not to admire it, necessarily, but some knowledge of his creativity allows for more objective criticism.

To think of Gray only as a nineties' poet, furthermore, is not quite proper. Gray's gifts, as Ian Fletcher has pointed out, survived into the twentieth century and were fulfilled. Fletcher's admiration for Gray the poet has encouraged him to collect all of Gray's verse and to plan for its eventual publication. Only after all his poetry is collected in one volume, Fletcher maintains, will readers and critics be able to deal with "a quietly compelling identity," to formulate a clearer idea of Gray's achievement.[6]

Much of the poetry that Gray wrote in the twenties and thirties, especially that found in *The Long Road* and *Poems (1931)*, compares favorably with that written by some of the better-known so-called moderns. That Gray had his own individualized styles, and cannot be conveniently categorized, is to his credit.

Several Grays followed one another through the decades. The poet who wrote *Silverpoints*, for example, does not at all resemble the poet who composed *The Blue Calendars*; nor does he closely approximate the poet who decade after decade seemed to find another voice. Oversimplification is so often falsification that to label him with one catch term or another is misleading. Geoffrey Grigson, nevertheless, likes to think of Gray as "less of a naturalist in the weak Georgian sense than a fantast in search of a hard style."[7]

In addition to one or two admirable short stories, Gray the writer of fiction did complete two noteworthy novellas. Neither *The Person in Question* nor *Park* has attracted more than a handful of readers, however. Nor is it likely that Gray will be remembered for his essays. His dramas do not stand a good chance of ever being republished. Much of what Gray wrote will remain curiosity pieces. All that being said, it is amazing how many of Gray's poems and examples of his prose have been published since his death in 1934. Dozens of his poems have been reprinted in anthologies and journals.[8] So, too, have *The Person in Question* and *Park* been posthumously published.

The few critics who have focused on the lasting quality of the best of Gray's work have good reasons for their views; still, what Gray's reputation may be fifty years from now, even they are not willing to conjecture. A fair-minded estimate allows the inference that Gray will not be soon forgotten, that his life, works, and influence will continue to attract more and more scholars.

The critic Geoffrey Grigson may overstate his case a bit when he writes glowingly of some of Gray's poems, especially "The Flying Fish," which he labels "one of the good 'modern' poems of our century"; but there is no refuting his judgment that Gray is "one of the half-hidden poets who cannot be left out of this century's account."[9] Every indication is that the memory of John Gray will more than merely linger—it should increase.

Notes and References

Chapter One

1. In 1961, under the editorship of Brocard Sewell, The *Aylesford Review* devoted its spring issue to several articles on John Gray and André Raffalovich. Two years later, these articles and several more made up a symposium edited by Sewell, which he entitled *Two Friends: John Gray and André Raffalovich* (Aylesford, 1963). In the same year, Gregory Grigson accorded Gray a full-page notice in his *Concise Encyclopedia of Modern World Literature* (New York: Hawthorne). In 1968, Sewell published his *Footnote to the Nineties: A Memoir of John Gray and André Raffalovich* (London). Interest in the life and works of Gray has been steadily increasing year by year.

2. To protect Gray's reputation, a year after his death, the Dominican Provincial, Fr. Bernard Delany, commissioned Dr. Helen Trudgian to write an official biography. She agreed to do so, but other commitments and failing health compelled her to abandon the project. Her notes and documentation were passed to Brocard Sewell through the kindness of her nephew, Peter Trudgian.

3. In 1966, Gray received a measure of attention through the prominence of his name in the Aubrey Beardsley Exhibition presented by Brian Reade at the Victoria and Albert Museum.

4. Their unique friendship is covered by Sewell, "John Gray and André Raffalovich: A Biographical Outline," in *Two Friends*, pp. 7–49.

5. Patricio Gannon, "John Gray," *Aylesford Review* 4 (Spring 1961):49.

6. It is quoted in Sewell, *Footnote to the Nineties*, p. 4.

7. The lecture was published in a condensed version in *Albemarle* 2 (July 1892):20–24.

8. *Daily Telegraph*, February 12, 1892.

9. Ibid., February 20, 1892.

10. *Star*, February 6, 1892.

11. Raymond Roseliep, "Some Letters of Lionel Johnson" (Ph.D. diss., University of Notre Dame, 1954), p. 109.

12. Desmond Flower and Henry Maas, eds., *The Letters of Ernest Dowson* (London: Cassell, 1967), February 2, 1891, pp. 182–83.

13. G. F. Sims Catalogue No. 25: item 145.

14. Donald Hyde Collection, New York, N.Y.

15. Brian Reade in his *Sexual Heretics: Male Homosexuality in English Literature, 1850–1900* (London: Routledge & K. Paul, 1970) resolves the question by suggesting that Gray probably had "no strong sexual inclination at all," but rather "a kind of incipient sexual anaesthesia" (p. 34).

16. In his *Uranisme et Unisexualité: Etude sur Differentes Manifestations de L'Instinct Sexuel* (Lyons: Storck, 1895), Raffalovich amplifies the dichotomy (cf. pp. 5–30). He published his study in France, for the entire subject was taboo in England, especially after Wilde's notorious trials. *Uranisme et Unisexualité*, being a pioneer work, caught the attention of psychologists. Havelock Ellis, for one, thought highly of Raffalovich's work and quoted from it in his own *Psychology of Sex*, which was published in America in 1897 and brought him an unsought-for notoriety.

17. Alexander Michaelson [pseud. of Raffalovich], "Oscar Wilde," *Blackfriars* 8 (1927):702.

18. *Star*, February 15, 1892.

19. Ibid.

20. Robert Sherard, for one, appears in *Dorian Gray* as Sir Anthony Sherard. Displeased with the use of his name in the novel, Sherard requested Wilde to remove it. For reasons known only to Wilde, he refused to honor his friend's earnest request. See Sherard's *Bernard Shaw, Frank Harris, and Oscar Wilde* (London: T. Werner Laurie, 1937), pp. 154–55.

21. Rupert Croft-Cooke, *Feasting with Panthers* (London: W. H. Allen, 1967), p. 209.

22. Jerusha McCormack, "The Disciple: John Gray/ 'Dorian' Gray," *Journal of the 1890s*, nos. 5 & 6 (1975–76), p. 14.

23. Rupert Hart-Davis, ed., *The Letters of Oscar Wilde* (New York: Harcourt, Brace, World, 1962), p. 249.

24. Isobel Murray, *Introduction to The Picture of Dorian Gray* (London: Oxford, 1974), p. x.

25. *Star*, May 2, 1892.

26. Ibid., February 6, 1892.

27. Flower and Maas, eds., *Letters of Ernest Dowson*, July 5, 1896, pp. 371–72.

28. From a letter of Gray's to one of Marmaduke Langdale's sisters, quoted by Sewell in *Two Friends*, p. 9.

29. Oscar Wilde, *The Picture of Dorian Gray* (Baltimore, Md.: Penguin, 1968), p. 147.

30. Ibid., p. 155.

31. Ibid., p. 148.

32. Uncatalogued letter from Gray to Raffalovich, February 10, 1899; Dominican Chaplaincy, Edinburgh. Jerusha McCormack, in "The Disciple," p. 14, recommends that the course of sin was "an initiation into sexual—and specifically, homosexual experience."

33. Wilde, *Picture of Dorian Gray*, p. 149.

34. Flower and Maas, eds., *Letters of Ernest Dowson*, October 15, 1893, pp. 294–95.

35. Uncatalogued letter, Dominican Chaplaincy, Edinburgh.

36. An unsigned review of *Silverpoints*, in the *Artist and Journal of Home Culture* (April 1, 1893), p. 119, noted "Mr. Pater, Mr. Swinburne and Mr. Theodore Watts have praised the 'Silverpoints' of Mr. John Gray."

37. Letter from Gray to Louÿs, November 27, 1892, quoted by Rogert A. Lhombreaud, "Arcade Ambro: The Poetical Friendship of John Gray and Pierre Louÿs," in *Two Friends*, p. 126.

38. This interesting question was first asked by Brocard Sewell after he learned of the incident from William Muir (Sewell, *Footnote to the Nineties*, p. 43).

39. *Universe*, May 26, 1961.

40. The priest was Father Dominic Hart. See his "Some Memories of John Gray," *Innes Review* 26 (1975):81–88.

41. Peter F. Anson, "Random Reminiscences of John Gray and André Raffalovich," in *Two Friends*, p. 135.

42. Ibid.

43. Edwin Essex, "The Canon in Residence," in *Two Friends*, p. 154. p. 154.

44. Ibid.

45. Ibid.

46. *Blackfriars* 15 (1934):405–7.

Chapter Two

1. *Dial* 1 (1899):10.
2. Ibid.
3. Ibid., p. 9.
4. Ibid., p. 10.
5. Ibid., p. 12.
6. Ibid., p. 10.
7. Rupert Croft-Cooke, captious of virtually everything Gray wrote, carped that the essay was written in "an enthusiastic schoolboyish way" (*Feasting with Panthers*, p. 209). Alexandra Zaina, on the other hand, who was more receptive to what Gray was trying to say, labels the critique "judicious and penetrating" ("The Prose Works of John Gray," in *Two Friends*, p. 71).
8. *Dial* 1 (1889):14.
9. Ibid.
10. Ibid., p. 15.
11. Ibid., p. 16.
12. Ibid., p. 17.
13. Ibid., p. 18.
14. Ibid.
15. "Garth Wilkinson," *Dial* 3 (1893):23.
16. An uncatalogued letter, dated January 11, 1893, from Wilkinson to Gray in the Dominican Chaplaincy, Edinburgh, confirms their meeting.
17. "Garth Wilkinson," p. 24.
18. Ibid., p. 23.
19. Ibid.
20. "The Redemption of Durtal," *Dial* 4 (1896):7.
21. Ibid.
22. Ibid., p. 10.
23. Ibid., p. 11.
24. Croft-Cooke claims that André Raffalovich's mother entertained such figures as Sarah Bernhardt, Colette, Robert Louis Stevenson, Mallarmé, and Huysmans at her Paris *salons* (*Feasting with Panthers*, p. 223). If indeed Huysmans was a guest at Madam Raffalovich's home, it is possible that Gray met him there.
25. "Trois Lettres Inédites de A. Raffalovich à J.-K. Huysmans," in *Two Friends*, p. 192.

26. Ibid.

27. A Gray devotee, Dom Patricio Gannon, came across "The Person in Question" in 1957. The story aroused his curiosity. Well aware that much of Gray's fiction was autobiographical, Gannon began to wonder what light "The Person in Question" might throw into some of the dark corners of Gray's life. Troubled with questions and intrigued with his discovery, Gannon arranged for the publication of Gray's story in a limited edition of forty numbered copies, with an additional ten copies for the press. To give an authentic nineties flavor to the edition, he selected a Beardsley drawing, *Garcons de Cafe*, for a frontispiece.

In March 1958, "The Person in Question" was published in Buenos Aires by F. A. Colombo. There was no demand for a second edition, not even for a limited run of fifty copies; but in 1971, the story did reach many more readers when it was reprinted in the winter issue of the *Antigonish Review*, pp. 67–75. Of interest is a prefatory note that Gannon wrote in which he gave a brief description of Gray as poet and dandy. He indicated that "The Person in Question" contains a clue to the motives leading Gray to renounce the worldly success that lay within his grasp. Since Gray's curious piece of fiction also provides a gloss of sorts on Wilde's *Dorian Gray*, Gannon related Gray's story to Wilde's novel and discussed parallels found in both works.

28. "The Person in Question," *Antigonish Review* 1 (1971):68.

29. Ibid., p. 69.

30. Ibid., p. 71.

31. Ibid., p. 75.

32. Ibid.

33. Ibid.

34. Ibid.

35. "The Café Royal," in *The Café Royal and Other Essays* (London: C. W. Beaumont, 1923), p. 4.

36. Letter from Raffalovich to William Rothenstein, Houghton Library, Harvard University, Cambridge, Mass.

37. Ibid.

38. *Times* (London), June 18, 1894.

39. Clement Scott, "The Playhouses," *Illustrated London News* 104 (June 1894):766.

40. *Theatre* 24 (July 1, 1894):37.

41. Ibid., p. 38.

42. A fine presentation copy, inscribed by Gray to William Roth-enstein (with his bookplate), is in the Berg Collection, New York Public Library. The publication is so rare, however, there is apparently no copy in the British Museum.

43. *A Northern Aspect. The Ambush of Young Days. Two Duologues* (London [?]: Privately printed, 1895), p. 6.

44. Ibid., p. 7.

45. Ibid., p. 29.

46. Ibid., p. 40.

47. Ibid.

48. Sewell, *Footnote to the Nineties*, p. 34.

Chapter Three

1. Gray to Lane, May 27, 1892, Berg Collection, New York Public Library.

2. Gray to Lane, June 18, 1892, Berg Collection, New York Public Library.

3. Introduction to *A Bibliography of Books Issued by Hacon and Ricketts* (London: Ballantyne Press, 1904), pp. vi–vii.

4. Ibid., p. vii.

5. See Denys Sutton," A Neglected Virtuoso: Charles Ricketts and His Achievements," *Apollo* 83 (1966):138–47.

6. Most studies that allude to *Silverpoints* state that Wilde paid the costs of publication. During his research into the archives of the Bodley Head, James G. Nelson discovered otherwise. See his article, "Footnote to the Nineties," *Times Literary Supplement*, September 18, 1969, p. 1026. In his book *The Early Nineties: A View from the Bodley Head* (Cambridge, Mass.: Harvard University Press, 1971), p. 95, he states the terms of the revised contract. The original contract is in the general manuscript collection of Princeton University Library, Princeton, N. J.

7. Gray to Lane, June 18, 1892, Berg Collection, New York Public Library.

8. It was first printed by John Gawsworth in *Known Signatures* (London: Rich & Cowan, 1932) along with "Sound," pp. 54–56.

9. Paul Winckler of Long Island University, C. W. Post Center,

Greenvale, New York. He contributed an interesting essay, "John Gray and His Times," to *Two Friends*, pp. 1–6.

10. On July 22, 1952, Sr. Mary Raphael wrote to the British Museum to protest the attribution of "Sound" to her brother. She received a deferential reply from C. B. Oldham, principal keeper of printed books. "It is almost certainly not by your brother," he replied, "though I regret to say that it still appears as one of his works in our general catalogue." Oldham did not explain why he arrived at this conclusion, but he added: "I have not yet identified the author for certain with any other John Gray . . . though I am inclined to think he may be the John Gray who published an autobiography entitled *Gin and Bitters* in 1938." (Sr. Mary Raphael's letter and C. B. Oldham's response are in a collection of Gray material that she turned over to Paul Winckler.) But Ian Fletcher, in a letter dated June 6, 1976, first called my attention to the manuscript copy of "Sound." In his opinion, "there is no doubt about its authenticity." The poem, which is in Gray's own hand, is now in the Princeton University Library.

11. *Graphic* 47 (April 8, 1893):383.

12. *Pall Mall Gazette* (May 4, 1893):3.

13. Richard Le Gallienne, *The Romantic Nineties* (New York: Doubleday, 1925), p. 101.

14. Quoted in Violet Wyndham, *The Sphinx and Her Circle* (London: A. Deutsch, 1963), p. 105.

15. Robert Hitchens, *The Green Carnation* (New York: D. Appleton, 1894), pp. 41–42.

16. Ibid.

17. Gray first met the princess in London at a dinner in her honor sponsored by Frank Harris, to which he invited Wilde, George Moore, and other men of letters. When the dinner was over, Gray was requested to read some of his poetry. Later, the princess wrote to Gray to thank him and to express her reaction to his recitations: "I was most enthusiastic. They carried me far away." See Robert Sherard, *The Life of Oscar Wilde* (London: T. Warner Laurie, 1928), p. 297.

18. Linda Dowling, "Nature and Decadence," *Victorian Poetry* 15 (1977):165.

19. Ibid.

20. Baudelaire in his *"Eloge du Maquillage"* had pointed out, as Gray knew, the connection between cosmetics and morals, that whereas crime is natural, virtue is artificial, so the application of make-up is a praiseworthy attempt to rise above the natural.

21. Ian Fletcher, "The Poetry of John Gray," *Aylesford Review* 4 (Spring 1961):64.

22. Jerome Buckley, *The Victorian Temper* (Cambridge, Mass.: Harvard University Press, 1951), p. 236.

23. William York Tindall, *Forces in Modern British Literature* (New York: Knopf, 1947), p. 245.

24. Fletcher, "Poetry of John Gray," p. 63.

25. Nelson, *Early Nineties*, p. 202.

26. Dowling, "Nature and Decadence," p. 164.

27. Ibid., p. 167.

28. Ibid.

29. Ibid.

30. Daniel de Graaf in *Arthur Rimbaud* (Assen Pays-Bas: Van Gorcum, 1960), pp. 20–21, claims the poet had not seen Millais's painting before he composed his poem.

31. Quoted in *Two Friends*, pp. 126–27.

32. This is also the opinion of C. Chadwick. See his edition of *Sagesse* (London: Athlone Press, 1973), p. 86.

33. George Moore, *Confessions of a Young Man* (London: Heinemann, 1952), p. 62.

34. A. E. Carter, *Paul Verlaine* (New York: Twayne, 1969), p. 60.

35. Arthur Symons also translated both of these poems for *Knave of Hearts* (London: Heinemann, 1913). His translation of "Clair de Lune" is commendable; but as Ruth Temple has noted, his rendition of "Spleen" is "less good than John Gray's translation, which does use the octosyllabic verse of the original" (*The Critic's Alchemy* [New York: Twayne, 1953], p. 150).

36. See Sewell, *Footnote to the Nineties*, p. 17.

37. Gray's translation is superior to most others that have been attempted. Aldous Huxley's is a very close second to Gray's, however. See Huxley's "Femmes Damness" in *Arabia Infelix and Other Poems* (London: Chatto & Windus, 1929).

38. Arthur Symons, *Les Fleurs du Mal* (New York: Boni, 1925).

39. Temple, *The Critic's Alchemy*, p. 143.

Chapter Four

1. Ian Fletcher, "The Poetry of John Gray," in *Two Friends*, pp. 59–60.

2. Olive Custance, *Opals* (London: John Lane, 1897). The book contains the poem "Ideal," written for Gray. Her volume *Rainbows* (London: John Lane, 1902) also contains three more poems dedicated to Gray, "Reminiscences," "Ritornello," and "The Silence of Love," holographic copies of which are in the Berg Collection, New York Public Library.

3. The letter is quoted in full in Sewell, *Footnote to the Nineties*, p. 16.

4. Flower and Maas, eds., *Letters of Ernest Dowson*.

5. Henry Maas, J. L. Duncan, and W. G. Good, eds., *The Letters of Aubrey Beardsley* (London: Cassell, 1970).

6. The volume, complete with Lady Gregory's unique bookplate, is in the Berg Collection, New York Public Library.

7. Fletcher, "Poetry of John Gray," in *Two Friends*, p. 62.

8. Osbert Burdett, *The Beardsley Period* (London: John Lane, 1925), p. 166.

9. Ibid., p. 167.

10. Flower and Maas, eds., *Letters of Ernest Dowson*.

11. A sonnet to St. Sebastian is found in Gray's *Blue Calendar* for January 1897. Raffalovich also shared Gray's fondness for St. Sebastian. When he was baptized into the Church of Rome, Raffalovich changed his name from Marc-André to André-Sebastian. Wilde, too, it is interesting to note, had an interest in St. Sebastian. He used the saint's name in one of his early poems, "The Grave of Keats" (1877), and for a short time after his release from prison in 1897, he used the alias Sebastian Melmoth.

12. See especially the letters dated May 5, May 7, May 13, October 21, and October 31, 1897, in Maas et al., eds., *Letters of Aubrey Beardsley*.

13. See Campbell's "Upon a Gloomy Night," in *Collected Poems*, vol. 3 (Chicago: Regnery, 1960), pp. 47–48; Nim's "The Dark Night," in *The Poems of St. John of the Cross* (Chicago: University of Chicago Press, 1979), pp. 19–21; and Peers's "Poems" ("Songs of the Soul"), in *The Complete Works of St. John of the Cross* (Westminster, Md.: Newman, 1945), pp. 441–42.

14. Flower and Maas, eds., *Letters of Ernest Dowson.*

15. Maas et al., eds., *Letters of Aubrey Beardsley.*

16. Ibid.

17. Ibid.

18. Quoted by Roger A. Lhombreaud in "Une Amitié Anglaise de Pierre Louÿs: Onze Lettres Inédites à John Gray," *Revue de Litterature Comparee* 27 (Juillet-Septembre 1953):354.

19. The first two are in D. H. S. Nicholson and A. H. E. Lee, eds., *The Oxford Book of Mystical Verse* (London: Oxford University Press, 1917), pp. 571–77; the third, in Thomas Walsh, ed., *The Catholic Anthology* (New York: Macmillan, 1932), p. 345, and in R. K. R. Thornton, ed., *Poetry of the Nineties* (Harmondsworth, Middlesex: Penguin, 1970), pp. 110–11.

20. Fletcher, "Poetry of John Gray," in *Two Friends*, p. 63.

21 Only one article has been written on Gray's religious poetry, and that by an anonymous author. See "Spiritual Decadence? Some Religious Poetry of John Gray," *Antigonish Review* 39 (Autumn 1979):89–95.

22. Maas et al., eds., *Letters of Aubrey Beardsley.* Whether Gray and Raffalovich did not care to have Beardsley illustrate their play or if Beardsley failed to follow through is not known, but *The Northern Aspect* was not illustrated.

23. See letters dated May 13 and May 25, 1895; and June 6, September 16, and December 12, 1896 in Maas et al., eds., *Letters of Aubrey Beardsley.*

24. Uncatalogued letter, Dominican Chaplaincy, Edinburgh.

25. Stanley Weintraub echoes the charge in *Beardsley: A Biography* (New York: Braziller, 1967), p. 101.

26. Malcolm Easton, *Aubrey and the Dying Lady: A Beardsley Riddle* (London: Secker & Warburg, 1972), p. 162.

27. Ibid.

28. See Yeats's *Memoirs* (New York: Macmillan Co., 1955), p. 91.

29. Maas et al., eds., *Letters of Aubrey Beardsley.*

30. Uncatalogued letter, Dominican Chaplaincy, Edinburgh.

31. Ibid.

32. Robert Ross, *Aubrey Beardsley* (London: John Lane, 1909), p. 171.

33. Ibid.

34. Maas et al., eds., *Letters of Aubrey Beardsley.*

35. Ross, *Aubrey Beardsley,* p. 172.

36. John Gray, *The Last Letters of Aubrey Beardsley* (London, 1904), pp. v–vi.

37. Ibid., pp. vii–viii.

38. Ibid., p. 155.

39. Ibid., p. ix.

40 Arthur Symons, *Aubrey Beardsley* (London: J. M. Dent, 1905), p. 173.

41. Holbrook Jackson, *The Eighteen Nineties* (New York: Capricorn Books, 1966), p. 94.

42. Isobel C. Clarke, "The Last Days of Aubrey Beardsley," *Thought* 7 (1933):553.

Chapter Five

1. In July 1899, Gray had been admitted into the Third Order of St. Dominic; at the time he took the name Brother Albert, after St. Albert the Great, the Dominican archbishop of Cologne. Raffalovich had been admitted into the Dominican Third Order in May 1898; at the time he took the name of Brother Sebastian. As tertiaries, Gray and Raffalovich were lay associates of the Dominican Order. Their association with the Dominicans afforded them several privileges and imposed certain obligations. It was probably through the Third Order that they first met another convert and tertiary, the sculptor Eric Gill.

2. See a letter of Raffalovich dated September 16, 1930, in Brocard Sewell, ed., "Letters of André Raffalovich to Edward Playfair," *Antigonish Review* 1 (1971):56.

3. See Leon Edel, *Henry James: The Master, 1901–1916* (London: Rupert Hart-Davis, 1972), pp. 416–17.

4. See Brigid Brophy, *Prancing Novelist: In Praise of Ronald Firbank* (London: Macmillan, 1973), pp. 274, 275, 278, 284, 308, 462.

5. Geoffrey Grigson, *Concise Encyclopedia of Modern World Literature,* (New York: Hawthorne, 1963), pp. 150–51.

6. The printing, which was done at St. Dominic's Press, Ditchling, Sussex, was restricted to seventy-five copies and went virtually unnoticed. Even Lady Margaret Sackville, to whom Gray dedicated the work, apparently failed to express her appreciation. In an article she wrote about Gray and Raffalovich, "At Whitehouse Terrace," she

made several interesting comments on their personalities, but she had little to say about Gray the poet—other than to remark, "His poetry, I fear, eluded me" (*Two Friends*, p. 146).

7. A copy of the prepublication issue, which was printed in Edinburgh by S. Walker, is in the Berg Collection, New York Public Library.

8. Quoted by Sewell, *Two Friends*, p. 40.

9. Fletcher "Poetry of John Gray," *Aylesford Review*, p. 70.

10. Quoted by Sewell, *Two Friends*, p. 40.

11. Edwin Essex, "The Canon in Residence," in *Two Friends*, pp. 160–61.

12. *Blackfriars* 8 (1927):127.

13. Ibid., p. 128.

14. Fletcher, "Poetry of John Gray," *Aylesford Review*, p. 70.

15. *Blackfriars* 8 (1927):27.

16. John Masefield, *A Sailor's Garland* (London: Methuen, 1906), pp. 18–26. Masefield also included Gray's "Wings in the Dark" (from *Silverpoints*), p. 6.

17. *Blackfriars* 10 (1929):779–85. The author of the essay is given as Alexander Michaelson, a pseudonym used by Raffalovich.

18. Ibid., p. 782.

19. Ibid., p. 783.

20. Ibid.

21. Ibid., p. 784.

22. Ibid.

23. Ibid.

24. Ibid.

25. Geoffrey Grigson, "Dorian Gray: John Gray," in *The Contrary View* (London: Macmillan & Co., 1974), p. 177.

26. Grigson, *Concise Encyclopedia*, p. 150.

27. Grigson, "Dorian Gray: John Gray," p. 179.

28. Ibid.

29. Gray's library was filled with copies of the works of most twentieth-century poets. See Anthony D'Offay's *Books and Autograph Letters Mainly of the Eighteen-Nineties: John Gray and André Raffalovich* (London: July 1961).

30. Blunden to Gray, February 16, 1933; Dominican Chaplaincy, Edinburgh.

31. See Brocard Sewell, ed., "Some Memories of John Gray by the Reverend Dominic Hart," *Innes Review* 26 (1975):83–84.

32. In 1925, Gray published a brief description of St. Peter's Church and its furnishings. See his *St. Peter's, Edinburgh: A Brief Description of the Church and Its Contents* (Oxford: Basil Blackwell).

33. Sewell, ed., "Some Memories of John Gray," p. 84.

Chapter Six

1. *Blackfriars* 12 (1931):682–95; 13 (1932):45–51; 13 (1932): 158–63; 13 (1932):231–42.

2. This odd fact about Gray's missing teeth is pointed out by Alexandra Zaina in her essay, "The Prose Writings of John Gray," in *Two Friends*, p. 95.

3. John Gray, *Park* (London: Sheed and Ward, 1932), p. 89.

4. Ibid., p. 71.

5. Ibid, p. 125.

6. Ibid.

7. Ibid., p. 128.

8. Ibid.

9. Quoted by Sewell, *Footnote to the Nineties*, p. 83.

10. Gray, *Park*, p. 39.

11. Ibid., p. 18.

12. Ibid, pp. 80–81.

13. Bernard Bergonzi, "John Gray," in *The Turn of the Century* (London: Macmillan & Co., 1973), p. 118.

14. Zaina, "Prose Writings," p. 97.

15. Sewell, "John Gray and André Raffalovich: A Biographical Outline," in *Two Friends*, p. 44.

16. "Life With Pater," Times Literary Supplement, July 14, 1966, p. 620.

17. Ibid.

18. Ibid.

19. J. G. Ballard, "Notes from Nowhere," *Manchester Guardian*, July 1, 1966, p. 9.

20. John Pope-Hennessy, "Park," *Blackfriars* 14 (1933):65.

21. Sewell, *Footnote to the Nineties*, p. 84.

22. Zaina, "Prose Writings," p. 99.

23. Ibid., p. 98.

24. Bergonzi, "John Gray," in *Turn of the Century*, p. 118.

25. Ibid.

26. A second edition of *Park*, edited by Bernard Bergonzi, was published in 1966. Limited to 350 copies, it was printed by Gordon Norwood for the publisher, St. Albert's Press of Aylesford, Kent.

27. Walter Shewring, "Two Friends," in *Two Friends*, p. 150.

28. Zaina, "Prose Writings," p. 86.

29. John Gray, "God-Made and Machine-Made," *Blackfriars* 5 (1924):451–57.

30. An excellent treatment of this interesting subject is found in Herbert Sussman, *Victorians and the Machine: The Literary Response to Technology* (Cambridge, Mass.: Harvard University Press, 1968).

31. John Gray, "God-Made and Machine Made," p. 457.

32. John Gray, "Winter Walking," *Blackfriars* 6 (1925):148–53.

33. Ibid., p. 152.

34. John Gray, "Excursions," *Blackfriars* 7 (1926):80–85.

35. John Gray, "An Island Cloud-Factory," *Blackfriars* 7 (1926): 370–75.

36. Ibid., p. 374.

37. John Gray, "The Parting Guest," *Blackfriars* 10 (1924):786–90.

38. Ibid., p. 788.

39. John Gray, "Cyder," *Blackfriars* 8 (1927):499–504.

40. Ibid., p. 502.

41. John Gray, "André Raffalovich," *Blackfriars* 15 (1934):405–7.

42. Ibid., p. 406.

Chapter Seven

1. Quoted by Ezra Pound, "Lionel Johnson," in *Literary Essays*, ed. T. S. Eliot (New York: New Directions, 1968), p. 367.

2. Flower and Maas, eds., *Letters of Ernest Dowson*, p. 58.

3. Frank Harris, *Oscar Wilde, His Life and Confessions* (1916; reprint ed., East Lansing: Michigan State University Press, 1959), p. 73.

4. See Violet Wyndham, *The Sphinx and Her Circle: A Biographical Sketch of Ada Leverson* (New York: AMS Press, 1967), p. 105.

5. Sewell, ed., "Some Memories of John Gray," p. 81.

6. Fletcher, "The Poetry of John Gray," in *Two Friends*, p. 69.

Fletcher's edition of Gray's poetry will be published by C. & A. Woolf of London.

7. Grigson, *Concise Encyclopedia*, p. 196.

8. See G. A. Cevasco, "John Gray: A Primary Bibliography and an Annotated Bibliography of Writings about Him," *English Literature in Transition* 19 (1976):49–63.

9. Grigson, *The Contrary View*, p. 182.

Selected Bibliography

PRIMARY SOURCES

1. Poetry

Poems, 1931. London: Sheed & Ward, 1931.

Silverpoints. London: E. Mathews & J. Lane, 1893. Reprint. London: Minerva Press, 1973.

Sound. A Poem. London: Curwen, 1926.

Spiritual Poems. London: Hacon & Ricketts, 1896.

The Blue Calendar, 1895. London: privately printed, 1894.

The Blue Calendar, 1896. London: privately printed, 1895.

The Blue Calendar, 1897. London: privately printed, 1896.

"The Flying Fish." *Dial,* no. 4 (1896), pp. 1–6.

The Fourth and Last Blue Calendar, 1898. London: R. Folkard & Son, 1897.

The Long Road. Oxford: Basil Blackwell, 1926.

Vivis. Ditchling, Sussex: St. Dominic's Press, 1922.

2. Fiction

Park: A Fantastic Story. London: Sheed & Ward, 1932. Reprint. Aylesford, Kent: St. Albert's Press, 1966.

"The Great Worm." *Dial,* no. 1 (1889), pp. 14–18.

The Person in Question. Buenos Aires: privately printed, 1958. Reprint. *Antigonish Review* 1 (1971):267–75.

3. Essays

"Allanwater." *Blackfriars* 8 (1927):298–303.

"André Raffalovich." *Blackfriars* 15 (1934):405–7.

"An Island Cloud-factory." *Blackfriars* 7 (1926):370–75.
"Aubrey Beardsley." *La Revue Blanche* 16 (1898):68–77 [in French].
"Charter Alley." *Blackfriars* 9 (1928):30–34.
"Cyder." *Blackfriars* 8 (1927):499–504.
"Dods." *Blackfriars* 7 (1926):80–85.
"Excursions." *Blackfriars* 7 (1926):80–85.
"Garth Wilkinson." *Dial*, no. 3 (1893), pp. 21–24.
"God-made and Machine-made. *Blackfriars* 5 (1924):451–57.
"Les Goncourts." *Dial*, no. 1 (1889), pp. 9–13.
"October." *Blackfriars* 8 (1927):688–93.
"The Modern Actor." *Albemarle* 2 (1892):20–24.
"The Parting Guest." *Blackfriars* 10 (1929):786–90.
"The Redemption of Durtal." *Dial*, no. 4 (1896), pp. 7–11.
"Winter Walking." *Blackfriars* 6 (1925):148–53.

4. Drama

Gray, John, and Raffalovich, André. *A Northern Aspect* and *The Ambush of Young Days*. London: privately printed, 1895.

5. Translations and Edited Works

Fifty Songs by Thomas Campion. London: Hacon & Ricketts, 1896.
Last Letters of Aubrey Beardsley. London: Longmans, Green, 1904.
Nimphidia and the Muses by Michael Drayton. London: Ballantyne Press, 1896.
The Poems and Sonnets of Henry Constable. London: Hacon & Ricketts, 1897.
The Poems of Sir John Suckling. London: Ballantyne Press, 1896.
A Saint and Others. London: J. R. Osgood, McIlvaine, 1892. Four short stories of P. C. J. Bourget translated from the French.
St. Gertrude's O Beata Trinitas. London: Sheed & Ward, 1927. Reprint. 1928, 1936. Prayers of St. Gertrude and St. Mechtilde translated from the Latin.
The Sonnets of Sir Philip Sidney. London: Ballantyne Press, 1898.

SECONDARY SOURCES

1. Bibliographies

Cevasco, G. A. "John Gray (1866–1934): A Primary and an Annotated Bibliography of Writings about Him." *English Literature in Transition* 19 (1976):49–63.
Fletcher, Ian. "Amendments and Additions to a Bibliography of John
Gray." *English Literature in Transition* 20 (1979):62–67.

2. Books, Parts of Books, and Articles

Anonymous. "Spiritual Decadence? Some Religious Poetry of John
Gray." *Antigonish Review* 39 (1979):89–95. Focuses on Gray's
Spiritual Poems.
Anson, Peter F. "Random Reminiscences of John Gray and André
Raffalovich." In *Two Friends*. Edited by Brocard Sewell. Ayles-
ford, Kent: St. Albert's Press, 1963, pp. 134–41. An exploration
in some detail of the forty-year friendship of Gray and Raf-
falovich.
Bergonzi, Bernard. "John Gray's *Park*." *Alyesford Review* 7 (1965):
206–15; Reprint. "John Gray" in Bergonzi, *The Turn of the
Century*. London: Macmillan, 1973, pp. 114–23. Discussion of
the novella to illustrate its singular flavor.
"Canon John Gray." *Times* (London), June 19, 1934, p. 16. Obituary
article.
Croft-Cooke, Rupert. "Wilde, Gray and Raffalovich." *Feasting with
Panthers: A New Consideration of Some Late Victorian Witers*.
London: W. H. Allen, 1967, pp. 191–226. Details the friend-
ship between Wilde and Gray.
Dowling, Linda. "Nature and Decadence." *Victorian Poetry* 15 (1977):
159–69. Focuses on Gray's *Silverpoints* as an icon of the fin de
siècle.
Essex, Edwin. "The Canon in Residence." In *Two Friends*, pp. 152–66.
Covers Gray's priestly duties at St. Peter's Church, Edinburgh.
Fletcher, Ian. "The Poetry of John Gray." In *Two Friends*, pp. 50–69.

Favorable treatment of Gray's verse; considers influence of Baudelaire and other French poets.

Gannon, Patricio. "John Gray: The Prince of Dreams." *Aylesford Review* 4 (1961):43–49. Reviews the personal and literary highlights of Gray's life during the nineties.

Gawsworth, John. "Two Poets 'J. G.'" In *Two Friends*, pp. 267–72. Concerns a correspondence between Gawsworth and Gray.

Grigson, Geoffrey. "Dorian Gray/John Gray." In *The Contrary View*. London: Macmillan & Co., 1974, pp. 177–83. Lively discussion of Gray as a poet with favorable words about his "Flying Fish."

Hart, Dominic. "Some Memories of John Gray." *Innes Review* 26 (1975):80–85. Focuses on Gray's life as priest and poet in Edinburgh.

McCormack, Jerusha. "The Disciple: John Gray/'Dorian Gray.'" *Journal of the Eighteen-Nineties Society*, nos. 5 & 6 (1975–76), pp. 13–21. Interprets Gray as Wilde's disciple.

McLaren, Moray. "A Fantastic Story." *Tablet* (London) 220 (1966): 1356. Favorable discussion of Gray's *Park*.

Michaelson, Alexander [pseud. of André Raffalovich]. "Parallels." *Blackfriars* 10 (1929):779–85. Traces parallels between individuals Gray knew and allusions to them in his "Flying Fish."

Pope-Hennessy, J. "Park." *Blackfriars* 14 (1933):64–66. Discussion of *Park*, its appeal and limitations.

Sewell, Brocard. *Footnote to the Nineties: A Memoir of John Gray and André Raffalovich*. London: C. & A. Woolf, 1968. A joint biography.

————. "John Gray and André Raffalovich." In *Two Friends*, pp. 7–49. Explores the friendship of Gray and Raffalovich.

————. "On Re-Reading *Park*." *Aylesford Review* 7 (1965):215–18. An appraisal of Gray's novella.

Temple, Ruth Z. *The Critic's Alchemy: A Study of the Introduction of French Symbolism into England*. New York: Twayne, 1953, pp. 141, 147, 149–50, 322–23, 326, 329. Treats of the part that Gray played in the reception of French Symbolist writers into English literature.

Winckler, Paul A. "John Gray and His Times." In *Two Friends*, pp. 1–6. Maintains that though Gray was part of the aesthetic movement of the nineties, he never became completely immersed in it.

Zaina, Alexandra. "Prose Writings of John Gray." In *Two Friends,* pp. 70–90. Asserts that Gray's prose is as worthy of consideration as his poetry.

Index